# THIS HAPPY GIFT OF TONGUES

JIM DAVIDSON

# This Happy Gift of Tongues

Vine Publishing
Aberdeen
Scotland

Vine Publishing Ltd
2a Eden Place, Aberdeen AB2 4YF
Scotland

© Jim Davidson 1985

First published 1985

British Library Cataloguing in Publication Data
Davidson, Jim
This happy gift of tongues
1. Glossolalia
I. Title
248.2'      9 BLSH

ISBN 0 947599 02 9

Unless otherwise stated, quotations from the Bible are from the Authorized version. The quotation marked 'Amp.' refers to scripture taken from the AMPLIFIFED BIBLE, Old Testament. Copyright © 1962, 1964 by Zondervan Publishing House. Used by permission.

Set in Times

Printed in Great Britain by
Collins, Glasgow

# Contents

Dedication:
To Jean – my fellow-adventurer

# CHAPTER ONE

# How it began

This book really begins on a spring morning in 1968 in the small Scottish town of Penicuik where my wife, Jean, and I were the Salvation Army captains. We had been converted in Billy Graham meetings in 1955, and given ourselves to God for whatever He wanted to do with us. In 1958, that meant our going to train for Salvation Army officership. God had blessed our ministry in The Salvation Army, but at times its demands were too much for our resources. And those were the times we longed for the power which Jesus had promised His disciples.[1]

I'd read about the Pentecostal experience in the Book of Acts. I'd heard about tongues and the other gifts of the Spirit in the church today. I'd preached on being baptized or filled with the Holy Spirit, but was never satisfied with my own sermons. According to the Bible, there had to be more than what I had. I wanted to share the experience of the early-days Christians in the Acts of the Apostles. Surely, being filled with the Holy Spirit was more than simply dedicating myself to God? Surely the Holy Spirit did something in the Christian – something which empowered his ministry?

I wanted to be filled with the Spirit, and whenever someone preached about it, I listened hopefully. But it all seemed empty words. I wanted to have this experience, but no one was telling me how to get it.

Perhaps the fault was in me. Was I blocking it? Over the years, as the longing grew, so did the frustration. What was I doing wrong?

But through all that time, these words of Jesus encouraged me:

*'Ye shall receive power after that the Holy Ghost is come upon you.'*[1]

Jesus said that to His disciples, and I was a disciple. I had been called to go and preach the Gospel. Jean and I and our children were going to Hong Kong in the summer of 1968 on missionary service. If anyone needed the power of the Holy Spirit, I did.

I needed the power of God, not only to lead people to the Lord, and to do the everyday work of a Salvation Army officer – but to LOVE – and to keep my experience of the Lord fresh and real.

And so to that spring morning in 1968, when I went out visiting folks who attended the corps. The fields and gardens were bursting with new life. It was a bracing day, the kind of day you feel something good and new is going to happen, an optimistic day.

I came to a quiet street of cottages with neat gardens and trim lawns. Mrs Cunningham lived in one of these with her daughter and son-in-law since she had moved from Dunfermline when she became too frail to live on her own.

She was a lovely Christian who came to the 'Army' because there was no Pentecostal church in our town. For months she had been attending our meetings, but recently, illness had kept her indoors, so my visit was to pray with her and bring her comfort from the Bible. But God had planned something else for me that day.

I was with her for about ten minutes when she suddenly asked if I wanted to be baptised with the Holy Spirit. I was surprised, but something in me leapt in response.

'Yes,' I managed to blurt out, 'yes – I want very much to be baptised in the Holy Spirit.'

She smiled as if she had been expecting that answer. 'Then I'll pray for you,' she said.

I didn't wait to weight the pros and cons of what I was about to do. There and then I knelt on the rug by the fireside, and she laid hands on my head and prayed for me to be baptised with the Holy Spirit. Praise God – I'm glad I humbled myself to kneel before this old lady – this beautiful woman of God. I was the officer – I was supposed to do the ministering – but that day I knew what I needed, and I was determined I was going to get it, no matter what it cost me. I wanted that power which Jesus had promised.

Whatever I expected, whether it was tongues of fire or of voice, or both – I didn't get it. Nothing unusual happened. But I did feel happy; there was a wonderful lightening of my spirit. I had the assurance I'd done right.

It's not easy for a minister of religion to kneel and let someone else pray for him –

especially if it's not a fellow-minister . . .

and it's a woman . . .

an old woman . . .

who isn't even a member of his church or denomination.

But my hunger for God's blessing blotted out these objections.

A few days later I was in Officers' Councils, an annual conference for Salvation Army officers from throughout Scotland. It was held that year in the College of Education, Hamilton: I don't recall seeing students so it must have been their vacation time.

The meetings were challenging and inspiring: God was

blessing us. Then late in the final meeting, an opportunity was given for those who longed for more of God's love in their lives to come forward and rededicate themselves to God.

'That's for me,' I thought, and went forward.

I wasn't thinking of Mrs Cunningham's prayer or her laying hands on me. But I was ready for anything God asked of me, or wanted to give me. I went to the front of the hall and knelt.

Kneeling there in prayer, I gave myself afresh to God. Then I went back to my seat.

That was when it happened . . .

There was a physical sensation like warm water pouring over me, flooding me, drenching me. I had a wonderful uplifting of my spirit. I was overwhelmed with how wonderful God is – Jesus surpassed description – I just wanted to love Him, to praise Him, to shout aloud His Name. But I kept silent because I knew that if I began to speak out my feelings and my love, I'd make such a noise it would disturb everyone else.

The praise that longed to burst from me – it couldn't be confined by the strictures of my own language. It needed a freedom my ability in English could not give. What was straining behind my vocal organs was a language I did not understand – and if I had spoken out then, it would have been in tongues.

At that time I didn't know The Salvation Army disapproved of speaking in tongues. I learned later that the official policy was that tongues were not for nowadays: there were those who said – unofficially – that the tongues of today were from Satan. But those views have been modified in the 1980s, and tongues are now permitted for private use, but not to be used in public.

So I kept my tongues bottled up inside me until I

returned to the privacy of my room, simply because I didn't want to draw attention to myself or to disturb others in their worship. But once in my room, I lost myself in adoring God. I spoke in tongues – I prayed and praised – don't ask me how I knew the difference, but I knew all right – I don't know for how long, but even today, so many years later, I still thrill to that first experience.

Then I told others about it. I even preached in Salvation Meetings about it – I was so naive I didn't know I was doing wrong. On one occasion, in the Sunday morning service of a holiday weekend – the congregation was smaller than usual – after I had preached about being filled with the Spirit, I closed the meeting in prayer. But no one moved. I thought the congregation hadn't understood – so I prayed again, emphasising that the meeting was over. We should all go home. Still, no one left.

It was only then – I was slow on the uptake – I realised what was happening. I asked those who wanted to be baptised in the Holy Spirit to come forward and I would pray for them and lay hands on them. The whole congregation came out to the front. Only one old lady remained in her seat, lost in praise – Mrs Cunningham.

When they had all been prayed for, they went home. Such was the hunger among those Christians for the power of the Holy Spirit in their lives.

Jean and the children and I went overseas a few weeks later. I believe our going away saved me at that time from the folly of my naivety.

That autumn in Hong Kong, Jean also received the filling of the Holy Spirit and she spoke in tongues and praised God. It happened in a prayer meeting of the Society of St Stephen, a group led by Rick and Jean Stone Willans, and Jackie Pullinger of the Walled City. Now my wife I were both filled with the Spirit, and spoke in tongues. Our prayer life and love for people and the Bible surged with renewed life.

Being filled with the Spirit made our preaching more pointed and effective – it's easier to bring a message from God when you feel Him there beside you on the platform or in the pulpit. But we had never yet used any of the gifts of the Spirit listed in 1 Corinthians chapter 12, though we did pray privately in tongues.

Then things came to a head when the wife of our Buddhist gatekeeper fell ill. Leung Sap was admitted to a private hospital, and terminal cancer was diagnosed. Expenses were heavy, and The Salvation Army generously paid half the costs. Leung Sap then transferred to the Queen Mary Hospital, a Government hospital which gave free treatment to those in a low-income bracket.

One Thursday evening, during a prayer meeting, Jean and I felt we should visit Leung Sap in hospital, and that Jean should lay hands on her and pray for her healing. Next morning, we set off to the hospital at the south end of Hong Kong island.

I remember that journey only too well. Leung Sap had been moved to a convalescent hospital down by the sea so that she could be nourished and built-up in preparation for an operation. It meant we had to take two buses, and I was blaming Jean because we had missed the second one. It was a hot dusty walk of more than a mile. By the time we arrived at the hospital, I was in a cantankerous mood. But I also knew it was Satan trying to spoil something good, so I prayed through my misery and guilt.

And there were other complications:

We had never met Leung Sap before, so we wouldn't recognise her in a ward full of other Chinese ladies; and neither of us was fluent in Chinese, though Jean could converse a bit in the language of the market-place. But that hardly gave her the vocabulary for what she was about to do.

A nurse promised to introduce us to Leung Sap, and as we walked down the long ward, Jean was praying for guidance about what to say and how to say it in Cantonese. The Lord beautifully answered her.

When we came to Leung Sap's bed, the old lady looked at us, puzzled, but flattered by having two 'Gwai Los' – 'foreign devils' – visit her. It gave her 'face' with the other patients.

Jean launched out in faith in her Chinese. 'Good morning, Leung Sap. We are Captain and Mrs Davidson of The Salvation Army.' That was easy enough to start with – even I could say that in Cantonese.

The old lady, emaciated because of her illness and propped up in bed with pillows, nodded and smiled. Chinese are naturally polite with strangers.

'Do you believe in God?' Jean continued, obeying God's guidance.

Leung Sap inclined her head in assent.

Jean went on: 'Then Jesus said, "Believe also in Me."[2] Do you believe Jesus can heal you?'

Leung Sap nodded her head again. 'Hai, hai – Yes, Yes,' she said.

So Jean laid hands on her and prayed in the Name of Jesus for her to be healed. We left soon afterwards – there wasn't much in the way of conversation we could have with her – but before leaving the ward, we saw the ward-maid bringing in the trolley with the lunches. A few minutes later, Leung Sap ate her lunch with enjoyment, without the usual vomiting. That was the first time for many weeks she had managed to keep her food down.

On the following Tuesday when she was examined in the Queen Mary Hospital for an operation to insert a tube down her throat to help her feeding, the Catholic surgeon found there wasn't a trace of cancer in her body. He became excited, saying a miracle had taken place; the nurses were weeping with joy. He phoned our Centre with the good news. Leung Sap was not only healed, she had also accepted Jesus as her Saviour and Lord. And a few days later, her husband became a Christian too.

The healing came to the attention of our Salvation Army leaders in Hong Kong, and Jean and I came under suspicion. They thanked God for Leung Sap's healing, but forbade our having any more to do with the gifts of the Spirit, and especially with speaking in tongues. Not only should we not do them – at least in our capacity as SA officers – but we must never even mention the subject to Salvationists.

For the next ten years, Jean and I lived a double life: as officers of The Salvation Army, we were non-charismatic: as private citizens, Jim and Jean Davidson, we were active in the life and activities of the charismatic community of Hong Kong.

Then in late 1979, we felt God telling us that we must no longer live under this prohibition. We told our leaders that after that term of missionary service was concluded, we would exercise the gifts of the Spirit in our whole lives, including officership, just as the Holy Spirit led us in accord with the Bible's teaching. Our leaders asked us to resign but we refused because what we intended doing did not transgress Salvation Army doctrines – on the contrary, it was a natural extension of them. So our officership was terminated.

We parted from our brethren in The Salvation Army on terms of love and mutual respect. Our leaders kindly offered to extend our homeland furlough by an extra two months to help us settle back in Scotland, but it wasn't necessary. God supplied our needs. and now we were able to serve Him with a freedom we did not have before.

That's how it began for my family and me, and in the following chapters, I will show what the filling of the Holy Spirit has meant to us over the years – and what we've learned about this most maligned of gifts, which has been for us – 'this happy gift of tongues'.

*Text references*
1. Acts 1 verse 8.
2. John 14 verse 1.

# CHAPTER TWO

# Spiritual Bigheads?

Not every Christian agrees that tongues is 'a happy gift'. A retired minister of religion who once wrote me from Australia actually said it was 'a bad gift'. I tried to reason with him but since he never wrote again I don't know if he still feels that way.

That reminds me of what happened while I was visiting an old Christian friend a short time ago. We were talking about the Lord, when a pastor who was visiting the district called in to see him. Introductions over, the conversation on Christian things continued, and eventually moved on to what the Holy Spirit is doing in the church today.

The pastor obviously wasn't sympathetic toward the charismatic gifts but he was trying to be fair, and then he said: 'The trouble with the term "charismatic", is that it gives the impression that "charismatic" Christians think they are superior.'

It saddened me to hear that, because he was being sincere, and unfortunately, there may be some truth in it. It's easy to feel – 'I've got something from God the other Christians don't have.' And to go on and think that that makes me more important or superior or more favoured with God.

Satan loves Christians to be 'big-headed' about their 'spirituality'. The old joke – 'I used to be proud, but now

I'm perfect – ' is no joke when Satan makes it a pitfall for the Spirit-filled Christian. Anything good in me is of God – the glory is all His – not mine. If we remember that – and believe it – we don't get 'big-headed'.

Of course, being Spirit-filled does make me a better Christian – but better than what I myself used to be – not better than someone else.

My Christian life must not be compared with another Christian's, because what I am is uniquely me – how I respond to my circumstances, my weaknesses and strengths, my relationship with God, and so on. No two Christians are alike, so we cannot be compared with each other, at least not by someone who is not all-knowing: and only God is that.

The only comparison permitted is with my own 'before and after' self. Then I can testify to what God has done in me. I know a man who is not a Christian who is naturally more kind than I am. Yet I also know that God has taken from me my heart of stone and given me instead a heart of flesh. I know that He is working in me all the time getting me to think twice before responding harshly, and most of the time getting me to respond in love. But I long for the day when all my responses will be loving ones. That's comparing self with self – not with someone else.

Which brings me to an important truth:

One of the purposes of tongues is to build up the spiritual life of the speaker.[1]

The gifts of the Spirit don't make you superior to other Christians, but they do improve what you are. They are from God, and any experience of the Holy Spirit has to be beneficial, because He is love and He acts in love.

For myself, speaking in tongues stirs up my awareness of

the Holy Spirit and helps me climb above my circumstances. I may be on a patform or in a pulpit waiting to preach, and all I have to do is to pray quietly in tongues for a few moments and the sense of God's nearness comes to me, so that when I stand up, I can see this church or hall and those rows of people as part of God's eternal plan. It's as if praying in tongues brings me close to the gates of heaven, so that I'm more aware of God's reality than the material reality of the situation. Or I could be in trouble and feeling downcast, then praying in tongues brings me God's joy and peace.

Another criticism by those who are against the charismatic gifts is to say something like: 'You keep the gifts – I'd rather have the fruit.' They refer to these fruit of the Spirit:

' – the fruit of the Spirit is love, joy, peace, long-suffering, gentleness, goodness, faith, meekness, temperance: against such there is no law.'[2]

And another text is where Paul, after speaking of the Spirit's gifts, goes on to say:

' – and yet shew I unto you a more excellent way.'[3]

He says that this more excellent way is love, without which all the gifts – including the gift of tongues – are valueless. Love is the best way.

But to say: 'Let's have the fruit of the Spirit – not the gifts!' reveals a basic misunderstanding of what God is about. The fruit of the Spirit should not be contrasted with the gifts of the Spirit:

' – the word of wisdom – the word of knowledge – faith

*– gifts of healing – the working of miracles – prophecy – discerning of spirits – kinds of tongues – interpretation of tongues –* '[4]

The Bible does not say we must choose between the gifts of the Spirit or the fruit of the Spirit.

*The Bible says we should have both gifts and fruit!*

If a Christian experiencing the gifts is not showing the fruit, that isn't an argument against the gifts. But it does show that God the Holy Spirit can take ordinary and unsatisfactory material and work through them to God's glory.

A new Christian can be filled with the Holy Spirit[5], and speak in tongues. On the other hand, the fruit of the Spirit are the results of gradual spiritual growth. If you grow anything from seed, you know how long it takes for the green shoots to appear through the ground, and then months pass before the fruition. Fruit grows slowly. The growth is imperceptible, and yet on looking back, you can trace the development. So it is with the fruit of the Spirit.

While on the other hand, gifts are suddenly given. When someone presents you with a gift, one moment you don't have it, the next you do. So are the gifts of the Spirit.

However, a gift of the Spirit does have an effect on the Christian who uses it. It strengthens his faith. It is easier for him to believe in God and to be aware of God, to love God's word and to desire to obey God. And these things help a growth in grace and fruit.

Another criticism is that charismatic Christians think they are better than all the great servants of God in the past who did not speak in tongues. But the charismatic Christians must never compare themselves with any other Christian, past or present. Instead, they should thank God for all His servants, especially for those who have helped many people down the centuries to become Christians.

So what about those Christians who never spoke in tongues? Were they not filled with the Holy Spirit?

My own experience when I was first filled with the Holy Spirit taught me much. From the beginning, I was able to keep silent because I didn't want to disturb others, and I've been able to keep silent on many occasions since. As the Bible says: ' – *the spirits of the prophets are under the speaker's control* – '[6] So the Spirit-filled Christian can suppress his tongues. He can keep silent when he wishes to – or he can speak in his own language instead. On occasion, this is a Biblical practice.[7] He can do it because God wants him to.

But there are other unbiblical reasons for suppressing tongues:

Perhaps he doesn't know they are from God.

Or everything he has been taught, all the traditions of his church, is against tongues.

So we have ignorance on the one hand, or prejudice on the other, silencing the gift of God.

Another cause of not using tongues may be that the Spirit-filled Christian is too shy or afraid to speak in tongues, even in private. That seems a contradiction in terms – a Spirit-filled Christian who is shy or afraid, but it can happen.

Eight years after I was filled with the Spirit, I was still unable to pray in tongues in the company of others. I was too self-conscious. Tongues warred with common-sense, or maybe it was the other way round. It was in 1976 after I had been attending a prayer meeting in Kowloon for a few weeks, that I realized my silencing of tongues was hindering the Spirit in my life. So I determined to break out of my dumb strait-jacket.

On a Saturday evening, sitting beside Jean on a bus on Hong Kong island, I overcame my shyness and prayed in tongues. She heard me. Hallelujah! I'd broken through. A few days later in a prayer-meeting, I obeyed God's prompting and brought a message in tongues.

From that breakthrough – and it was like freeing the ice which blocks the river – blessings flowed. My own life was revitalised, and the blessings flowed out and travelled round the world to touch my own family – visions, prophecies, words of knowledge, interpretations – the Spirit had freedom to use me. I saw the blessing reach out to churches and groups I had the opportunity to minister to.

How could God use me in this way? Was it because I was an outstanding and talented man of God? Far from it. I am just an ordinary man – and that's being honest, not modest – but the Spirit was allowed to use the little I had, and in His hands, a little goes a long way.

Finally, I read recently that probably half of the criticism of tongues is inspired by the Holy Spirit pointing out the falseness of many people's tongues.[8]

If that is true, it is serious. We who speak in tongues have to pay attention to this charge. But we must also beware in case it becomes a tool in Satan's hands to suppress our tongues – either for messages, or in prayer, or in any other use. On the contrary, criticism should strengthen our resolve to be more under the Spirit's guidance, and to consciously surrender our all – including our vocal powers – to Him, for Him to use to the glory of God.

The charge that some people use tongues falsely – they are of self rather than of God – should make us more on our guard to be 100 per cent for God. There are people who preach and teach from the Bible, not for the glory of God, but for their own glory or the propagation of a heretical doctrine. But that should never cause the servants of God to say:

'Therefore I will no more preach or teach from the Bible because there are those who do it falsely.'

The false use of tongues must make us more on our guard to use them wisely, and under God's control.

*Text references*
1. 1 Corinthians 14 verse 4.
2. Galatians 5 verses 22, 23
3. 1 Corinthians 12 verse 31.
4. 1 Corinthians 12 verses 8–10.
5. Acts 10 verses 44–48.
6. 1 Corinthians 14 verse 32 (Amplified Version).
7. 1 Corinthians 14 verse 28.
8. Foster, K. N. (1976) *'I believe in Tongues, but . . .'* Victory, Eastbourne, page 94.

# CHAPTER THREE

# Tongues is for real

At one time I was privileged to be an adviser to the Women Aglow in Hong Kong, so I had the opportunity to accompany Jean to one of their Seminars. Because it was held in the morning and afternoon, the delegates were together for lunch. At our table were four others, including an Indian lady, Leila, with her husband, Samuel. Over the meal, she told us of an experience she had had that morning. As best as I can, I'll let her tell it in her own words.

'This morning when I was praying about coming to these meetings, I wasn't very keen, but Samuel wanted me to come so I agreed. You see, I belong to the Christian Brethren in India, where we don't believe in speaking in tongues or any of those wild things. But I decided to give God a chance to prove if tongues were real, though I didn't think He would for I was sure they weren't.

'However, I made this bargain. If I hear two people speaking in tongues today – praising God in tongues – and they don't know the languages they are speaking, but I understand them, then I will believe tongues are genuine.

'This morning, the RAF gentleman who was sitting with his wife, stood and prayed in tongues. I checked that he did not know the language he was speaking, but I understood it. He was praising God in one of our Indian dialects. He could never have known it.

So I decided tongues is real and at the end of the meeting I received the baptism of the Holy Spirit and I have spoken in tongues too.'

'But you asked for two signs –' one of us reminded her.

She smiled. 'You're quite right I asked for two speaking in tongues – but one was enough. I know now – tongues is for real . . .'

We couldn't have agreed more, but not everyone would. Some people say that tongues are just made up by the speaker, and that is supported by the reference in the last chapter to 'false tongues'.[1]

Even some Christians who speak in tongues ask themselves:

'Is this real?' Even they find it incredible that God's Spirit should speak through them in this way. Especially at the beginning when it's new and unfamiliar.

But it is important we should have no doubts about this: tongues are genuine. We do not make them up: they are 100 per cent Biblical. Speaking in tongues has blessed and built up countless Christians in their faith. And through them, God has authenticated their experience by blessing many others, often miraculously.

When a Christian is used while he is praying in tongues to heal someone, and the healed one then glorifies God and accepts Christ as his Lord and Saviour, you can be sure that the Holy Spirit is in it. Satan doesn't want to see people healed and become Christians – he is not in the business of glorifying God.

There are those, however, who try to give an aura of scientific respectability to their criticism by saying that tongues are just a mix-up of the speaker's own language.

I was at university at the time when I read one such criticism in a book[2] on psycholinguistics. I had read other books and papers on the subject and some of them were also not encouraging. Terms such as: 'fabricated language',[3] 'abnormal and inarticulate vocal utterance',[4] and 'stream of meaningless syllables'[5] cropped up. That book on psycholinguistics[2] went so far as to lump Christian speaking in tongues along with the tongues of witch-doctors, spiritualist mediums, and people suffering from mental illness. According to the writer, tongues were just 'a special kind of transformation of language habits'.

But where was the proof for all these statements?

Studies had been done of the Eskimo witch-doctors or shamans of the arctic regions,[6] of the tongues of spiritualist mediums,[7] and of schizophrenics.[8] But I could find no study on the actual sounds produced in Christian tongues. So why were Christians lumped together with them? It sounded more like prejudice than science.

A psycho-linguist had said Christian tongues were merely 'a special kind of transformation of language habits'. That criticism seemed to be proved for the tongues of mediums and schizophrenics – there was some doubt about the shamans – but I could find no evidence put forward to back up what was said about Christian tongues. So I decided to do the research for my degree in psychology into whether or not tongues were 'a special kind of transformation of language habits'.

I began with the assumption that if tongues were just a rearrangement of a speaker's own language, then his tongues would have enough of his language in it to betray what language it was. That is what happened with mediums and schizophrenics. Would it happen with Christian tongues?

First, the Head of the Linguistic Department of Hong

Kong university was asked to listen to a tape-recording and say what he thought it was. It was a recording of an American minister speaking in tongues, but he wasn't told this.

His conclusion was that while he could not identify what language it was, he believed it was a regular language for it had the patterns of intonation and orderly sequence of sounds one would find in a real language. That was encouraging, fine as far as it went – but that wasn't enough. All it indicated was that Christian tongues – at least in this instance – were not just a random jumble of sounds borrowed from the speaker's own language. It could still be a stringing together of these sounds. On the basis of this finding, however, I was given the go-ahead by the university's Psychology Department to research the subject.

The first formal part of the research was to enlarge on that academic's opinion. Then I would try to find out if there were enough remnants of the speaker's native language for listeners to identify it in their tongues.

I recorded the tongues of fourteen Christians: they came from six language backgrounds:

| | |
|---|---|
| Chinese | American |
| Canadian | Scottish |
| French | English |

Armed with tape-recorder and tape to play back, I went round consulates and language centres. I found thirteen people who took the time to listen to the tape and give their opinions on what they heard. They were expert in a wide range of languages, including English, French, German, Spanish, Italian, Russian, Hebrew, Arabic and Chinese. They weren't told they were listening to tongues, but were asked simply to comment on what they heard, and if possible, to identify the speakers' nationalities.

Details of this and the remainder of the research will be found in the Appendix. But briefly, the findings were:

'It sounded like poetry in parts.'

Eleven of the thirteen judges thought that they were listening to real languages. The two judges who had doubts, still thought that some of them were real languages, such as:

'Hindu or African –'

'Arabian or Hungarian –'

'A SE Asian language –'

'Tamil –'

'A melodious native language.'

So far, unprejudiced listeners to tongues thought they were hearing real languages, and no one had said the tongues sounded like someone speaking a jumbled version of the speaker's native language.

But there was more to do before I could say there is evidence that speaking in tongues is more than the reassembled sounds of the speaker's own language. A number of factors may have influenced the judges' opinions.

They included the judges' unfamiliarity with the native language of the tongues' speaker, or that taking part in an experiment had 'unsettled' them.

To offset these and other possible objections, I decided to do a more detailed study, in which I would make allowances for the possible objections.

I began by recording the tongues of three young women: American, Chinese and English. For each woman, I wrote a transcript of her tongues. An example of the American's tongues is given here:

'Oleanda koli ishika ashama handa oleakekeranda karanda ashika ofea –'

This was then divided into separate sounds which were then jumbled up so that I now had a copy of the reassembled tongues. An extract of this reassembly is given here:

'Ekondorek ekarandom andea amaneshika enderafishana omeankondore –'

Then the speaker in tongues and two other of her fellow-countrywomen who didn't speak in tongues, practised the reassembled tongues until they could read it fluently as if speaking it. These were recorded on the same tape as the original tongues, so that I now had twelve different pieces of speech – three of tongues, and nine of reassembled tongues.

With this tape, I visited groups of people and played it over to them. They were told that three nationalities were represented: Chinese, English and American, and asked to identify the speakers' nationalities. Although the groups of listeners were multi-national, I used only the data of the English people for the English subjects, the American for the American, and the Chinese for the Chinese. In this way I ensured that the opinions of the English speaker in tongues were given by people who were familiar with her native language, and the same for the other two.

In this table given below, are the numbers of people who managed to identify their fellow-countrywoman's nationality from listening to her tongues, compared with those who couldn't.

|  | Chinese | English | American |
|---|---|---|---|
| Did recognise her nationality | 22 | 10 | 2 |
| Did NOT recognise it | 50 | 19 | 53 |

From these results, we can see that most Chinese and English did not recognise the nationality of their fellow-countrywoman when she spoke in tongues. This is significant, especially since they had only three languages to choose from.

But when we look at the results for the American speaker in tongues, her tongues were so different from her own language that hardly anyone thought she was American. This has to be strong evidence against those who say that tongues is merely speaking a reassembled concoction of your own language.

At this point, I could say that the research had shown:

(1) that some speaking in tongues sounded like real languages, and

(2) that in one of three examples of tongues studied (the American's), there was overwhelming evidence to support the view that speaking in tongues was not a rearrangement of the speaker's native language.

There was still one other study to do.

This was to pin-point any important differences between the speaker's native language and his speaking in tongues. A French priest agreed to cooperate with me on this, although he did not know in detail what I meant to do – simply that I was researching speaking in tongues. He could speak English and Chinese in addition to French, but his French accent was very strong, and even in these other languages, he emphasised certain syllables which are natural in French but out of place in these other languages.

What I wanted to find out were:

(1) Would his tongues have these emphasised syllables?

(2) Would his tongues have sounds which aren't in the French language?

The answer to the first question was an unqualified, 'No!'

There was a conspicuous shortage of emphasised syllables in his tongues, and one stressed syllable which always occurs in spoken French was absent in his tongues.

The answer to the second question was a 'Yes!' On thirteen occasions, his tongues produced double vowels or diphthongs which do not occur in French. Data on these findings are in the Appendix.

So once again, the evidence did not support those who say that Christian tongues are simply a 'special kind of transformation of language habits'. The evidence said plainly that tongues is not something we make up by using our own language.

There are two points we should consider before closing this chapter.

What about the tongues we sometimes hear which do bear a resemblance to the speaker's language?

I once visited Holland for a few days, and was intrigued by what I discovered when I did some window-shopping. The signs and posters looked alien to my eyes, but when I read them aloud, the sounds reminded me of my native Buchan dialect in the north-east of Scotland. I was even able to understand some of the words. And yet this was a foreign language to me.

So if Scots and Dutch have similar sounds, so may some tongues and our native languages, and yet still be independent of each other.

To close with: there are occasions when in a prayer in tongues you can hear the same sound over and over again – or even the same group of sounds, like a recurring phrase. But this does not mean it is not a real prayer. Just as it is possible in an English prayer, to hear something like:

'Wonderful Jesus, lovely Jesus, wonderful Jesus . . .'

To someone who did not understand English, that could sound like the repetition of meaningless sounds.

When we speak or pray in tongues, we must not be self-conscious about what we are saying. Let us fix our thoughts on the Lord and allow Him, through His Spirit, to guide our tongues and thoughts. He is well able to do that.

*Text references*
1. Foster, K. N. (1976) *'I believe in Tongues, but . . .'*.
2. Carroll, J. B. (1964) *'Language and Thought'* New Jersey: Prentice Hall.
3. Drever, J. (1965) *'A Dictionary of Psychology'* London: Penguin.
4. *Encyclopedia Brittanica* vol. 22.
5. Thouless, R. H. (1950) *'An Introduction to the Psychology of Religion'* Cambridge UP.
6. May (1956) *American Anthropologist* 58 pp. 76–9.
7. Flournoy, T. (1900) *'Des Indes a la Planete Mars'* and *Proceedings of Soc. Psych. Research* vol. 12.
8. Bobon, J. (1947) 'A contribution to the study of regressive phenomena in psychopathology' in *Jnl. Belge. Neurol. Psychiat.* 47. pp. 329–95.

# CHAPTER FOUR

## Satan's Counterfeit . . .

Anyone who says of a Christian: 'His tongues are not of God!' had better be sure of his facts. To go further and assert that they are of Satan is possibly the most hazardous thing he is every likely to say. The Pharisees said something like that when they criticised Jesus for healing a man possessed by a blind and dumb spirit:

> 'This fellow doth not cast out devils, but by Beezebub the prince of the devils.'[1]

People who say that any manifestation of the Holy Spirit – and tongues is a manifestation of the Holy Spirit – is of Satan, are in danger of being condemned as the Pharisees were:

> ' – whosoever speaketh against the Holy Ghost, it shall not be forgiven him, neither in this world, neither in the world to come.'[2]

But yet we have to acknowledge that Satan does counterfeit the works of God; he will even disguise himself as an angel. The Bible says:

> ' – Satan himself is transformed into an angel of light.'[3]

And he has his counterfeit of speaking in tongues. We already know that witch-doctors and Eskimo shamans speak in tongues. We already have heard of the tongues of mediums and schizophrenics. Speaking in tongues has its imitations, and this is one way by which Satan attempts to discredit the Holy Spirit's work in the church.

But just because Satan counterfeits a good sign from God doesn't mean we must reject that sign. What it means is that we have to be careful to test these signs, and the people who bring them. The church does not ban the preaching of the Gospel just because there are heretics who preach false gospels.

Two strangers once came to a united charismatic prayer meeting I attended weekly. They seemed very keen to be involved and to minister, to prophesy and to speak in tongues. But the leaders of the meeting gave the strangers no encouragement to minister for they felt uneasy in their presence – there was a feeling in our spirits which I may describe as a 'jangling' feeling. Something didn't feel right.

After the meeting we soon discovered why we were uneasy. The two men belonged to a church which said that Jesus Christ had returned a few years earlier as an American. According to them, Jesus died soon afterwards from natural causes, and these two were His sole representatives on earth – they were the entire church of Jesus Christ. All the rest of us were misguided by Satan.

The Holy Spirit within us had told us to beware of the men, and so we must always be on our guard against wolves who come to tear the flock.

However, if a speaker in tongues glorifies and praises God, and if he confesses that Jesus is come in the flesh,[4] and his life and beliefs are in agreement with what the Bible teaches, we should accept his tongues as genuine. We don't have to be in doubt about this, but if we are, it is better to err on the side of giving God the glory, rather than run the risk of blaspheming against the Holy Spirit.

Even if someone brings a false tongues' message, if we are filled with the Holy Spirit and under His control, he won't let us be led astray or into error. God is more powerful than Satan.[5]

Another criticism of tongues, and linked with the idea that they are Satanic, is to say that speaking in tongues causes mental instability. There is no real evidence to support this. It is based on prejudice, not on scientific fact.

In just the same way, the experience of being born again is said to cause mental upset . . .

I knew a young woman, a wife and mother, who had a nervous breakdown just days after she became a Christian, but it was revealed later that she had been under domestic strain for years. It had been building up in her, and the emotional experience of becoming a Christian had – as it were – lanced the boil. Her nervous breakdown was a safety-valve for releasing the mental pressure. She soon recovered, and because of the breakdown, her personal circumstances were improved so that she never had another.

There is a mistaken belief that when you speak in tongues, you 'are beside yourself'. That you are in a state of ecstasy, of withdrawal from reality. In the years since I first had the experience of speaking in tongues, I have moved constantly in charismatic circles, yet I have never seen anyone who could be described as 'beside himself', (except on television). Of course, I've seen Christians who were 'lost in wonder, love and praise' – I've been like that myself – but I was always aware of the external world in the background, I never lost control of myself, and I could come out of the experience at any time. Just as the young man is lost in love as he gazes into his beloved's eyes and she has agreed to marry him, and everything is wonderful. He could 'snap out of it' if he wanted to. But why should he? He's enjoying himself.

To translate tongues as 'ecstatic tongues' encourages this wrong idea. The speaker always has control of himself; he can start and stop his tongues as he wishes.[6] Recently I was speaking to the British leader of an international missionary society, and he was explaining why his society did not permit speaking in tongues among their members. During our conversation, he referred to 'ecstatic tongues'. That is not Scriptural. And experience does not support it. It is possible to speak in tongues without being in an exalted state of delight. Speaking in tongues does not depend on our feelings. We pray by faith, we bring messages by faith, and the Holy Spirit works through us.

The only serious research done – as far as I know – on the mental and emotional states of Christians who speak in tongues was at the University of Witwatersrand in South Africa. One of the findings was that speaking in tongues had a therapeutic effect if the speaker had previously been mentally disturbed. It made him more stable.[7]

A. A. Hoekema, in his book: 'What about Tongue Speaking?' considers the possibility of tongues being demonically instigated. He says:

' – whenever it causes bitter discord between Christians who ought to conduct themselves as one in Christ – surely the devil has a hand in the situation.'[8]

With equal truth, we may say that whenever there is bitter discord between Christians, regardless of the subject of the discord, the devil is there somewhere.

Christians have fought over baptism – over the Eucharist

or Communion meal or Lord's Supper (there isn't even agreement on what to call it) – over how a church should be governed – over the meaning of texts in the Bible. And when Christians fall out over these and other things – when Christians refuse to love another – then Satan is having an influence somewhere. But would we be justified in saying that baptism, and the Lord's Supper, or church government and the scriptures, are all demonically instigated? Or the various ways in which Christians handle them are of Satan?

· Christians are not perfect, and we do sometimes wrongly use God's gifts. The history of the Church, and our own experience, prove this. But we don't reject God's perfect gifts because of our faults.

Instead we must use whatever he gives us as He wants them to be used.

Being filled with the Spirit and speaking and praying in tongues is good for us. It is God's doing – it has to be good.

I know a young woman who is qualified in art. At college, she was talented, but shy. So shy in fact, that her tutor told her that her creative ability was being strangled by it. She couldn't break out of herself to express herself artistically. And her exam grades were suffering as a result.

Then at the conclusion of a Full Gospel Business Men's chapter meeting, she was filled with the Holy Spirit. She prayed and praised in tongues. From then on she was more free to express herself. Her tutor complimented her on the obvious improvement in her work, and she graduated successfully. She is still a shy girl, but her shyness no longer has the last word. God's Spirit has released her.

*Text references*
1. Matthew 12 verse 24.

2. Matthew 12 verses 31, 32.
3. 2 Corinthians 11 verse 14.
4. 1 John 4 verse 2.
5. 1 John 4 verse 4.
6. 1 Corinthians 14 verse 32.
7. Vivier, L. M. V E. (1960) *Glossolalia* unpublished doctoral dissertation, Library of Harvard School of Divinity (microfilm).
8. Hoekema, A. A. (1976) *'What about Tongue Speaking?'* Exeter, Paternoster. p. 127.

# CHAPTER FIVE

# A Model for Speaking in Tongues

What are we doing when we speak in tongues? If we confine our answer to what the Bible says, we have to say that in tongues, our spirit prays or bring messages from God, but our understanding is not involved. And that's it.

But if we may speculate and propose an explanation of what speaking in tongues is, an explanation which agrees with what we know from the Bible, then it may help us to understand some puzzling aspects of the phenomenon. I wish to suggest here one such model: I can not claim it is the only possible model, but it does fit the Biblical facts, and it borrows from what psycholinguists know about the development of language. It will also answer some questions which occur regarding speaking in tongues:

(a) How is it that witch-doctors, spiritualist mediums, and some patients suffering from mental illness, speak in a kind of tongues?

(b) How can those who were Christians but have since abandoned their faith, still speak in tongues?

(c) Why is it that some people who investigate speaking in tongues claim that they find many instances of false tongues – that is, speaking in tongues which is not of the Holy Spirit?

(d) Can a Christian speak in tongues and not be

thinking of God? That is, not be consciously co-operating with the Holy Spirit? And if so – how?

(e) How does man's spirit co-operate with the Holy Spirit in the speaking of tongues?

While it is not part of the model, a reason will also be suggested for why tongues should be the first sign of the filling of the Holy Spirit.

So let's look at the model, remembering that as with all scientific theories, it is just a suggestion, not a guaranteed explanation.

## *The Model*

Many psychologists and others working in the field of language development believe we are born with an ability to learn language – a language mechanism which is found only in humans. They express this theory in statements such as:

'– a fundamental capacity for language – '[1]
'– the child's inborn capacity for language – '[2]
Language acquisition ability which is – ' – reminiscent of the biological development of an embryo – '[3], and
' – his learning capacity – for language, being as inborn – '
' – highly restrictive characterisation of a class of generative systems (potential theories) from which the grammar of its language is selected – '[4]

and so on, which all imply we have this inborn language acquisition mechanism. In this model for tongues speaking, I will refer to this language acquisition mechanism by the abbreviation: LAM.

41

I was thinking of an analogy for LAM when I remember what happened when I took down the Christmas decorations. The concertina-like paper festoon, when I dropped it from the top of the step-ladder, automatically wanted to fold into a set pattern. So it is with LAM: when it encounters the right circumstances, it automatically works to form a language.

LAM converts ideas or thoughts into vocal symbols or words, and forms their relationship with each other so that they communicate our thoughts – that is, we speak to each other, and understand those who speak to us.

The form of relationship between the words, we call the rules of grammar. Here is an example:

*Words – or vocabulary items*

| Name words (nouns) | Describing words (adjectives) | Being words (verbs) |
|---|---|---|
| cat | black | is |
| dog | fierce | are |
| | the | |
| | a | |

*Grammar Rules*

(a) One or more adjectives may stand before a noun.
(b) The form of verb 'to be' may stand between a noun and a following adjective.

From these words and rules the following sentence is formed:

'The black dog is fierce.'

So with the words and rules initiated by LAM, language is formed – the significant operation of LAM being its continuing activity to give form and pattern to groups of

42

sounds so that their relationship with each other and with the real world they symbolise is recognised and acknowledged.

In one's early years, LAM has the capacity to promote any language known to man. This is demonstrated in the learning of one's native language.

LAM embraces memory, understanding and the speech area of the brain, but it is not synonymous with any or all of them. This may be represented thus:

*Diagram 1*

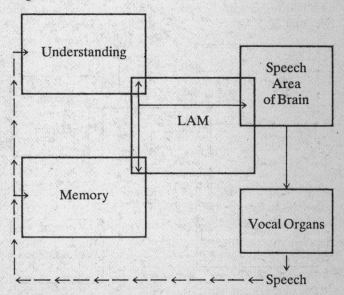

Understanding and memory are linked, one influencing the other, and it is they which through LAM activate the Speech Area of the brain. When we speak, we hear the sounds and they feed back to our understanding and memory. This is represented by the dotted line in Diagram 1.

When we speak in tongues, the Holy Spirit interposes, and His understanding and memory – if I may be permitted to speak of Him as if He had these human faculties – take the place of man's memory and understanding. We see this in Diagram 2:

*Diagram 2*

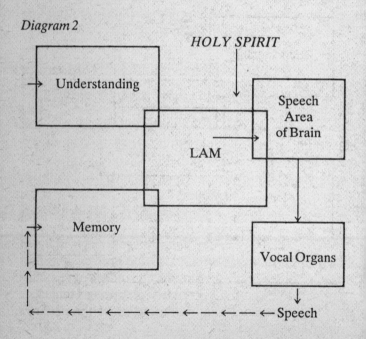

There is a feedback of the sound of the tongue to the memory but none to the understanding. In addition, since LAM has been operating in the production of a tongue, this tongue will exist in potential in the speaker from then on. When the Holy Spirit initiates the tongue, then it is a proper tongue, as it is when by faith, the Spirit-filled Christian prays in his tongue.

This could explain why once people get the ability to speak in tongues, they don't lose it, even if they abandon their Christian faith. But since the Holy Spirit would not be in it, it would be a meaningless activity.

LAM may also be activated by spirits other than the Holy Spirit if the individual opens himself up to them, as do shamans and spiritualist mediums, and members of some heretical sects.

The Bible says:

*'The gifts and calling of God are without repentance.'*[5]

The word for 'gift' is 'charismata', the same as in 1 Corinthians chapter 12 for the gifts of the Spirit. What it means is that when God calls and gives gifts, He does not take them back. That is why once you have the ability to speak in tongues, you always have it, although it is not really communicating messages or prayers unless the Holy Spirit provides the content.

In some forms of mental illness, the normal working of the brain is disturbed so that after the manner of a short circuit, the LAM may by-pass the understanding, drawing only on the memory store, and thus producing a tongue or pseudo-glossolalia which has fragments of the patient's native language.[6]

Why is tongues the first sign of being filled with the Holy Spirit?

Understanding is an essential part of an individual's integrity – his pride of being. We rebel against doing something if we are just told to do it; we want to understand why.

'If you explain, I'll do it. But don't ask me to obey blindly.'

That's a common attitude. And a useful one when you have to cope with life and its demands as an intelligent responsible being.

But when you have yielded yourself to obey another – in total obedience – dare I say: 'slavish obedience'? – then do you have to understand?

Speaking in tongues is a prime example of obeying without understanding. And added significance is given to such obedience when one remembers that the Bible says –

'– the tongue can no man tame.'[7]

No man can tame the tongue, our speech. But the Holy Spirit can; when man's spirit yields to Him the right to use all that he is.

And again, speech is arguably the highest form of co-operation between mind and body. Tongues spectacularly demonstrates the Spirit's control of them. In fact, speaking in tongues may be said to be the Holy Spirit celebrating God's coronation over His once unruly subject.

This model may be altered in future, but in the meantime, it helps to explain aspects of speaking in tongues. The gift of tongues, being able to pray in tongues, is good for us, whether or not it makes sense to us. If we can explain it – reverentially – to our own satisfaction in a way that has the backing of the Bible, and our own experience tallies with it, then that is an added bonus.

*Text references*

1. D. McNeill (1966) 'The Creation of language in children' in *Psycholinguistics papers*: J. Lyons and R. Wales (eds) Chicago: Aldine p. 99.
2. J. Katz (1966) *The philosophy of language* New York: Harper & Row.
3. R. Brown and U. Bellugi (1964) 'Three processes in Child's acquisition of syntax' in *New Directions in the study of Language* E. Lenneberg: Cambridge: MIT Press p. 161.
4. Noam Chomsky (1964) 'Current issues in linguistic theory' in J. A. Fodor. J. J. Katz (eds) *The Structure of language: readings in the philosophy of language*: Englewood Cliffs, N.J.: Prentice-Hall
5. Romans 11 verse 29.
6. Bobon, J. (ibid).
7. James 3 verse 8.

# CHAPTER SIX

# The Gifts . . .

Having fitted the gift of tongues into a psychological framework, we must now reaffirm its place in the Bible. Tongues is a gift included in the list of 'charismata' in 1 Corinthians chapter 12. If we look at the list and its context, we get a clearer picture of the significance of tongues.

However, the question of how important – or unimportant – tongues are should not arise, for none of us qualifies to pass judgment on what the Holy Spirit does.

That reminds me of a danger which can arise from a book like this: one devoted to the gift of tongues. And that is that readers may get the impression that tongues is the most important gift. That would be wrong, just as it is wrong to say it is the least valuable and least important.

However, for some inexplicable reason, tongues is the gift which draws most hostility to itself. Perhaps even those who are most against tongues, can't explain their antipathy.

To get a clear picture of what tongues means in the context of Spiritual gifts, we have to study the first eleven verses of 1 Corinthians chapter 12.

Paul wrote this letter against a background of a church which was infiltrated with wrong practices. Among these was an over-emphasis on speaking in tongues, and Paul had to tell the Corinthian Believers where they were going wrong, and how to correct it.

Why did they make so much of tongues?

One reason may have been that being able to speak well in public was highly prized among them. Had there been 'pop-stars' in those days, it's more likely they would have been orators rather than singers or musicians.

When he was in Athens, Paul went to the Agora or 'Open Space' for public-speaking – a cross between Hyde Park Corner and the Houses of Parliament. He tried to win the Athenians to Jesus by oratory and argument, but he failed. Only a few believed and it seems there was no church founded there.

From Athens, he went to Corinth, where it was a different story altogether.

> *'And I, brethren, when I came to you, came not with excellency of speech or of wisdom, declaring unto you the testimony of God . . . my speech and my preaching was not with enticing words of man's wisdom, but in demonstration of the Spirit, and of power.'[1]*

In Corinth, a lively church began. Paul remained there for eighteen months,[2] and had a successful ministry. But you only have to read his Corinthian letters to know there were many faults among the Christians. Much of the godlessness of the city – it was one of the busiest sea-ports of the ancient world, a place where east met west – infected the Christian fellowship. And although Paul preached in the power and authority of the Holy Spirit, his determination not to charm his hearers with clever speech, brought on him the disrespect of some of his hearers, so that he wrote in his second letter to them:

> *'For his letters (referring to himself), say they are weighty*

*and powerful; but his bodily presence is weak, and his
speech contemptible.'*[3]

Speech was important to the Greeks in another way. On
the south-eastern slopes of Mount Parnassus, was a temple
dedicated to the Greek god, Apollo. A female prophet
named Pythia lived and worked there, and when she was
in a state of frenzy, she uttered sounds, said to be the words
of Apollo. Temple priests interpreted these as divine
advice which was prized by the ordinary people and the
rulers.

There is one more thing to say about speech before we
go on to study this passage. To the Jews of Bible days, the
tongue was the most important part of a man by which he
could praise God, and some went so far as to say it was the
only part which could be used and inspired by God.[4] So to
both Jews and Greeks, speaking was important, and
especially in their religions.

*Verse 1: 'Now concerning spiritual gifts, brethren, I
would not have you ignorant.'*

The term 'spiritual gifts' is not accurate. The word for
'gifts' has been added in the English, and 'spiritual gifts' is
a translation of the Greek word: 'pneumatikai', which
really means 'spiritual things' or 'things of the spirit'.

Paul does not want his readers to be ignorant about the
things of the Spirit. For too long, the Church has paid lip-
service to the Trinity, whie giving little attention to the
Holy Spirit. Our God is Father, Son and Holy Spirit. And
we must give each the place in our lives which the Bible says
they must have.

*Verse 2: 'Ye know that ye were Gentiles, carried away*

*unto these dumb idols, even as ye were led.'*

'Carried away' describes an animal being led away, perhaps to the slaughter, or someone being taken into imprisonment.

What these Gentiles had been led or carried away to were 'dumb idols'. In the Old Testament, when the servants of God wished to show how useless the gods of the heathens were, they said they were dumb.[5] When Elijah challenged the priests of Baal to a duel to show which God was the true one, he said that they should call on their gods, and the God which answered by fire would be the true God. The priests called on their god for hours, but

*'There was no voice, nor any that answered.'*[6]

Often in the Bible there are instances of people hearing the voice of God:

Adam and Eve in the garden in the cool of the day;
Moses on Mount Sinai;
the child Samuel;
Elijah hearing the 'still small voice';
Isaiah in the Temple,

and in the New Testament,

Jesus at His baptism, and
Saul on the road to Damascus.[7]

God still speaks to us, usually in a silent voice within our mind, but sometimes, though very rarely, in an audible voice. On one occasion, I believe I heard God audibly. It happened like this:

Jean and I were commissioned in London as Salvation Army officers, and my father came down to be with us. On the Saturday evening, a meeting was held in the then Clapton Congress Hall, and at the end, when people were invited to go forward to commit their lives to Christ, I saw father sitting about ten rows from the front of the hall. I was alone in a small tunnelway leading from the backstage to the platform, wondering whether or not I should go and speak to him about going forward.

And then an audible voice behind me said:

'Go on!'

I turned to see who had spoken, but there was no one there. All the sounds were coming from the hall and platform; behind me the soundproof doors separating the tunnel from backstage were closed. There was no natural explanation for that voice and those words. So I took them to be from God, and I went down and spoke to father, and right then he surrendered his life to God.

I believe God spoke to me, and it doesn't matter if sceptics scoff and say: 'Rubbish!' I obeyed what I still believe was the voice of God, and my father found peace through Jesus Christ, and he had that peace for the rest of his life. One way or the other, God did speak, and as I obeyed, He was glorified and my father was blessed.

Our God is not a dumb fool. He desires to communicate with us. Let us have listening ears to the voice of God – but remember, an important component of 'listening ears' is a willingness to obey what He commands.

*Verse 3: 'Wherefore I give you to understand, that no man speaking by the Spirit of God calleth Jesus accursed: and that no man can say that Jesus is the Lord, but by the Holy Ghost.'*

' – no man speaking by the Spirit of God.' Apparently there were some who claimed inspiration by the Spirit to say certain things about Jesus. 'Very well,' said Paul, 'you can find out if they are led by the Spirit of God or by Satan, by what they say.'

And what did some of them say? It would appear that some were saying that Jesus was 'accursed'.

The word for 'accursed' is an interesting one. In the original, as 'anathema', it really means something devoted to or consecrated to a god. But in addition, it also means that what is consecrated cannot be redeemed or bought back, and that being sacrificed results in the complete destruction of the offering.

When the Old Testament was translated into Greek, Leviticus chapter 27 verse 28 had the word 'anathema' for the Hebrew word for 'devoted'. Jesus was a sacrifice, devoted to the doing of His Father's will, but He was not destroyed without trace. On the contrary, He had the power and authority to rise from the dead.

In fact, it was by His resurrection we know He is the Son of God,[8] and that His sacrifice on the cross was acceptable as the means of blotting out our sins and reconciling us to God. So anyone who said: 'Jesus is anathema', was really saying: 'Jesus was sacrificed and that was him finished, dead and gone. He could not have been Saviour and Lord, and certainly not the Son of God.'

No one could say that by inspiration of God's Spirit.

On the other hand, he who said: ' "Jesus is Lord!" would be saying what Thomas said when he saw the risen Lord.[9] This is what Paul said to the Believers in Rome:

'– if thou shalt confess with thy mouth the Lord Jesus, and shalt believe in thine heart that God hath raised him from the dead, thou shalt be saved.'[10]

To say: 'Jesus is Lord!' separates Believers from the unbelievers.

Paul wanted the Corinthian Believers to know the difference between those who were inspired by the Holy Spirit, and those inspired by another spirit. That had to be understood before he could teach them how the Holy Spirit acted through them; they had to be sure it was God's spirit, and not the kind of spirit which spoke through Pythia at the temple of Apollo.

What are these, the introductory verses of this chapter saying?

'I want you to know about the Spiritual things of which you asked. People who say that the cross finished off Jesus are not inspired by the Holy Spirit: people who confess that Jesus is the resurrected Lord are led to say that by the Holy Spirit.'

Verse 4: 'Now there are diversities of gifts, but the same Spirit.'

'Gift' is a translation of 'charisma' which means 'grace. favour or kindness'. Charisma or favour is shown by a superior to his inferior. It is used when God gives something good to men. An example is:

' – the gift (charis) of God is eternal life through Jesus Christ our Lord.'[11]

Verse 5: 'And there are differences of administrations, but the same Lord.'

'Administrations' is the translation of the word 'diakonia'. It is from that word we get the word 'deacon' and it means ways of serving someone, of carrying out

54

administration duties, or obeying commands. This is why the verse ends with the words: 'but the same Lord,' for it is a Lord who commands, and his servants who obey.

On to verse 6:

*'And there are diversities of operations, but it is the same God which worketh all in all.'*

That phrase 'God worketh all in all' presents a mental picture of God providing the energy or power ('worketh' = 'energon') for the electrical equipment, heating and light over a great district.

*Verse 7: 'But the manifestation of the Spirit is given to every man to profit withal.'*

The word 'manifestation' and the phrase 'profit withal' in this verse teach us a great deal. In particular, the word 'manifestation' is very significant.

It is the translation of the Greek word: 'phanerosis', which in turn is based on the word 'phanos' – a torch or light.

Just as a torch or light reveals things in the darkness, so the manifestation of the Holy Spirit reveals Him to us.

Two words are used in the New Testament for 'manifestation'. They are: 'apokalupsis', and 'phanerosis'.

From 'apokalupsis' we get 'revelation' as in the Book of Revelation. Scholars tell us that 'apokalupsis' is more to do with what you know in your mind, what you realise. When a cartoon character has a bright idea, a small electric light bulb glows above his head – Donald Duck has just had an 'apokalupsis'.

'Phanerosis', on the other hand, is how our senses become aware of something. Our hearing, eyesight, smell and taste are exercised in 'phanerosis'. This means that the Holy Spirit reveals Himself to our senses – not only to our mind. We don't have to imagine or conjure up thoughts of what He is doing; the evidence is there to see and hear, to feel and to touch.

In a meeting led by two Lutheran missionaries in Hong Kong, I saw a woman healed of back trouble. At a distance of less than twenty-four inches, I saw one of her legs stretch to the same length as the other. She was told the pain in her back would take a few days to settle down. That was on the Saturday afternoon, and by Monday, her pain had gone.

In that instance, the manifestation of the Holy Spirit was evident in working a miracle of healing. I had seen a 'phanerosis' of the Spirit.

'Profit withal' is the English for 'sumpheron'. If that were written 'sympheron' you would probably guess it meaning: 'symphony'. For it means to bring or contribute together so as to be profitable, just as the instruments of a symphony orchestra combine together to produce lovely music.

The manifestations of the Holy Spirit are given to Christians to be used by them in harmony for the whole body of the Church, so that all may profit, and their service blend as one complete entity. Just as each instrument with its own musical part is needed in producing that which the composer intended, so each of the Spirit's gifts is necessary for God's work to be done.

*Text references*
1. 1 Corinthians 2 verses 1–4.
2. Acts 18 verse 11.
3. 2 Corinthians 10 verses 9, 10.
4. Thayer (1976) *'Greek–English Lexicon'* Grand Rapids: Zondervan see 'Glossa: 2'.

5. Habakkuk 2 verses 18, 19; Psalm 115 verse 4, 5; Jeremiah 10 verse 5.
6. 1 Kings 18 verse 26.
7. Genesis 3 verse 8; Exodus 19 verse 19; 1 Samuel 3 verses 4f; 1 Kings 19 verse 12; Isaiah 6 verse 8; Matthew 3 verse 17; Acts 9 verse 4.
8. Acts 2 verses 22-24; Romans 1 verse 4; Romans 4 verse 25; 1 Corinthians 15 verse 3.
9. John 20 verse 28.
10. Romans 10 verse 9.
11. Romans 6 verse 23.

# CHAPTER SEVEN

## . . . of the Spirit

There are nine manifestations of the Holy Spirit in 1 Corinthians chapter twelve.

*Verse 8: 'For to one is given by the Spirit the word of wisdom –'*

'Logos sophias' – 'word of wisdom'. The word 'logos' has two meanings tied in with it: 'the thought in your mind' – and 'the word or words you say to show that thought.' This word of wisdom passes through your mind and understanding, and you know it is of the Holy Spirit.

'Wisdom' – this word 'sophia' may also mean 'intelligence'. We should desire it a great deal. In the Book of Proverbs we read:

*' – for wisdom is better than rubies; and all things that may be desired are not to be compared to it.'*[1]

It is the first item in the list of manifestations. Does that reference to it being most desirable mean it is most important? Of course not: we are not qualified to judge the relative merits of the gifts of manifestations of the Holy Spirit.

But if we had to give a name to the most important

expression of God in us, it would have to be 'love'. For love is not just a manifestation of the Holy Spirit; love is the very nature of God.[2] Love is the motivation – the driving force – behind the manifestations. If love is missing, the manifestations are noisy gongs and sounding cymbals. Without love, the person whose life reveals the manifestations of the Spirit is failing.[3]

It is the Spirit who gives us love:

'– *the love of God is shed abroad in our hearts by the Holy Ghost* –'[4]

The Holy Spirit shares out His gifts according to God's wisdom and plan; but every Christian gets His love. Like everything else God gives us, however, we must exercise it.

It's been said the gift of wisdom is like knowing how Jesus would handle a difficult situation – having the wisdom of God when you don't know what to do. I believe Jesus showed this wisdom when He answered the chief priests and scribes when they asked Him:

*'Is it lawful for us to give tribute unto Caesar or no?'*

If Jesus had said: 'Yes,' the Jews would have thought He was a traitor. But if He said, 'No,' then the Romans could have arrested him as a trouble-maker.

Instead, He led His questioners to say that the coin bore the image of Caesar, to which he countered: '*Render therefore unto Caesar the things which be Caesar's, and unto God the things which be God's*'[5]

While the Holy Spirit gives to every one different gifts according to God's will, yet it is possible for Him to manifest Himself in any way He will if the Christian is yielded to Him. What this means is that while a Christian may have the gift of the word of wisdom, yet the Spirit may on occasion work Himself through him by the gift of healing or some other gift. We cannot restrict the Spirit's manifestations to how we think they are distributed.

The reason I say this is that while I believe I do not have the gift of the word of wisdom, yet there was one occasion when I feel I exercised it. I was faced with a difficult situation, inherited from decisions made years before, and now it was my responsibility to deal with it and make the best of it. What I did would affect the lives and livelihood of others, and almost certainly the work of the Kingdom of God.

There seemed to be no ideal solution possible, but I brought it before the Lord. He told me what to do, what to say. It involved dealing with people in a loving, tactful way, and asking them to make sacrifices, and it was further complicated because I had to comply with Government regulations, while not antagonising a powerful Trade Union. God gave me the wisdom to handle it, to say the right things, and the outcome was good for everyone concerned. I believe God was glorified through it.

*Verse 8 continued: 'to another the word of knowledge –'*

We can say as some do that this knowledge refers to knowledge about God and the things of our faith. It probably does include that. But just as wisdom can mean the wisdom that Jesus would have had in a difficult situation, so this knowledge can be the knowledge that Jesus often displayed – supernatural knowledge.[6]

We must remind ourselves that this wisdom and knowledge are manifestations of the Holy Spirit, so we can have something which goes beyond human mental capacity without getting puffed up or proud. It is all the work of God.

Jean and I were praying with a group of young Christians; they were young in age and in experience. It was the first time we'd met some of them. Then God told me to pray an unusual prayer for one of the girls. I prayed and thanked God that He was going to heal her, and that through this healing she would find wholeness and holiness, and through her, healing would come to her mother.

I talked with her later on her own, and she said there was nothing wrong with her; she wasn't ill. So I told her the specific nature of the illness God had told me she had and He was going to heal her of it, an illness she was now suffering from. Then she admitted she had that illness, but had told no one of it because she was worried about it. She also said that her mother suffered from a similar complaint.

Now she was able to rejoice that God was going to heal her, both in body and mind, as she had been healed in spirit. And that through her, healing would come to her mother. Her faith had an uplift – or as the Bible says – she was edified and built up.

*Verse 9: 'To another faith by the same Spirit –'*

Every Christian has faith.

*'For by grace are ye saved through faith; and that not of yourselves: it is the gift of God.'*[7]

But some Christians get a special endowment of faith. Charles McInally is one such. He gave up his post in the University of Hong Kong to devote himself full-time to caring for homeless children from the city streets. He opened his home to them, then moved to a larger building in the countryside – and he did this without knowing where his money was coming from. Miracles of provision were an everyday occurrence in Charles' life. Like the morning when there was no food and he had about fifteen children and staff to provide with breakfast, not counting lunch and supper. He went and sat in his car to pray – and there on the passenger seat was an envelope with a hundred dollars in it.

Many years ago on a five-minutes religious broadcast on BBC radio, I heard this prayer:

'Lord, give us the faith to take risks in Thy name.'

That prayer has stuck with me ever since. The gift of faith – that kind of faith, gets results.

*Verse 9 continued: 'to another the gift of healings by the same Spirit.'*

'Charismata iamaton' – gifts of healings'.
The word 'iamaton' has two meanings in the Greek:

 (i)  the medicine, remedy or means of healing, and
(ii)  the healing itself

As an example of how God is willing to manifest Himself through Spirit-filled Christians, may I share the story of what happened on one occasion when my daughter, Ruth, and her friend, Martin, attended a Full Gospel Business Men's meeting in Edinburgh.

During the time of ministry at the end, the guest speaker invited any Spirit-filled Christians who had never laid hands on anyone for healing, to come forward and do so for those who came out for healing. Ruth and Martin went forward, and prayed – both in English and tongues – for a woman who suffered with back trouble and had one leg a little shorter than the other. When they laid hands on her, they both saw her shorter leg grow before their eyes to the same length as the other. She was physically healed and her back pains went.

*Verse 10: 'To another the working of miracles –'*

The word for 'working' is the same word we studied in verse 6 for 'operations', and refers to the 'energy' or 'inworking' of the Holy Spirit in accomplishing the miracles, the 'dunamis'. That is the word we get 'dynamite' and 'dynamic' from. Strictly speaking, it does not mean 'miracles', but 'mighty works' or 'works of great power'.

I am reminded of the Lutheran minister who was sacked by his denomination for bringing back to life a woman who had died in his church during a Sunday service. I have reason to thank God for that man, for it was in 1977 during one of his prayer meetings that my wife, Jean, was healed of cervical spondylosis. She had suffered for sixteen years, but since being healed in that meeting, has had mobility of her spine and freedom from pain.

Another miracle affected my family. It includes healing, but I believe something in addition to the gift of healings was involved.

Ruth had suffered conjunctivitis in both eyes for almost two months. The doctor's treatment made it bearable, but it wasn't being healed. Then Jean, my daughter-in-law Linda, and our granddaughter, Sarah, contracted the disease. Eventually I caught it.

By this time, we were on holiday some sixty miles from

where Paul and Linda and Sarah were living. It was just after Christmas, 1980.

On the last Monday of the year, I went to the doctor and was given ointment for my eyes. Tuesday morning, my eyes were worse than ever. I had to go shopping, so I asked Jean to lay hands on me for healing. She was washing the breakfast things at the time, so she dried her hands and I can still feel the hot dampness of her hands as she laid them on my head and prayed for me to be healed.

I didn't feel any better, and I was squinting through half-shut eyes as I drove into town. I parked near a chemist and was tempted to go in and buy dark glasses, but I refused because I believed God was going to heal me. In the store where I was shopping my eyes were very sore and again I was tempted to buy dark glasses, but I insisted that God was healing me, even if I didn't feel it. There was a long queue at the cash-out so I resigned myself to a long wait. About twenty minutes later I left the shop and instead of having to screw my eyes up in the wintry sunshine, I found I could see perfectly well. My eyes were healed.

But not only were my eyes healed – so were Jean's and Ruth's. And sixty miles away, Linda and Sarah were also healed. None of us has suffered conjunctivitis since.

It was a straightforward healing in my case, but for the others, I believe it was also the working of a miracle. It helps us to remember that God is all-powerful and free. He does not have to conform to a list written down in our language. That list of gifts is to help us understand what He is doing, but as far as He is concerned, He is free to do what He wishes, when, where and how He wishes. All He asks is our faith and co-operation.

*Verse 10 continued – 'to another prophecy'*. The Greek word 'propheteia' depends on two words: 'pro' meaning 'before' or 'in front of something'[8], and at other times meaning 'at a time before the present time'[9]; and 'faimi' – 'to bring forward into the light' or 'to reveal or divulge'. There are examples of prophecy in both the Old and New Testaments[10], when they mean revealing what is going to happen in the future. But it can also mean declaring or speaking something which can only have been known to the speaker by supernatural means.[11]

That is what the Pharisees meant when they said that if Jesus were really a prophet He would have known that the woman who washed and anointed His feet was a sinful woman: He would have had God-given knowledge.

So prophecy may mean both 'forth-telling' and 'fore-telling' – but what is told forth is a message from God. And not a second-hand one either.

Prophets in the Bible were special people. When the Israelite maid, servant to Naaman's wife, told her master who was suffering from leprosy that there was a prophet in Samaria who could heal him, she was not thinking of a preacher – but of a man of God.[12]

No one can take upon himself the mantle of prophet. It is God who chooses and equips the prophet. That's how it was in Old Testament days, and in the New – and that's how it is today.

The Jewish leaders were cautious about how they spoke of John the Baptist, and how they behaved towards Jesus,[13] because the ordinary people regarded them both to be prophets. When Jesus restored to life the son of the widow of Nain, the people said: 'a great prophet is risen up among us – God hath visited his people.'[14] The prophet was someone special.

The list of gifts God has given to the church, recorded in Ephesians 4 vese 11, does not say:

' – *apostles, preachers, evangelists, pastors and teachers –*

Why? Because the apostles, evangelists, pastors and teachers would all have had to preach on occasion – they were all preachers. But the list says: ' – apostles, prophets, evangelists, pastors and teachers – ' So we conclude that 'prophet' is not just another way of saying 'preacher'.

Today, the prophet is the Christian to whom the Holy Spirit gives a message which he must share with others. It may be as a sermon, or just a few words. But the message has to be from God.

We must not confuse preaching with prophesying. For it is possible to preach truth and yet not be the mouthpiece of God. And no amount of effort on the speaker's part, of pleading in prayer and sincere effort, can coerce God into speaking through him, if he is not chosen to prophesy. God does the choosing: man the obeying.

*Verse 10 continued: 'to another discerning of spirits.'*

This means being able to discriminate or judge between various spirits. 'Spirits' here can mean the types of evil spirits which attack men, or even live in them, but more likely it refers to spirits inasmuch as they inspired men to say certain things. The best example of this is:

*'Beloved, believe not every spirit, but try the spirits whether they are of God: because many false spirits are gone out into the world. Hereby know ye the Spirit of God: Every spirit that confesseth that Jesus Christ is come in the flesh is of God: and every spirit that confesseth not that Jesus Christ is come in the flesh is not of God: and this is that spirit of antichrist, whereof ye have heard that it should come;'*[15]

In this example, being able to discern spirits would mean being able to tell when someone who claims to bring a message from God really is doing so, or if it is a message of his own, or from an evil spirit.

*Verse 12 continued: 'to another divers kinds of tongues –*
*'*

The word 'divers' is spelt differently nowadays – with an 'e' at the end. It means: 'various kinds of tongues'.

A multitude of languages is available to the speaker in tongues, but it is the Holy Spirit who decides which tongue to use. Scholars have counted about 3000 languages now existing, excluding the many dialects within these languages. Some languages are spoken by many millions of people, while even more are spoken by small numbers, some only by a few hundreds.[16] Then there are languages which existed in past ages – or perhaps have yet to exist in the future. And according to 1 Corinthians 13 verse 1, angels also have languages. So 'divers' languages means a wide choice of languages is available for use by the Holy Spirit.

*Verse 10 continued: 'to another the interpretation of tongues.'*

If the Bible did not say that 'interpretation of tongues' is a gift of the Holy Spirit, critics would say that the idea of interpreting tongues came from the priests who interpreted the messages of Pythia on Mount Parnassus. They would say that interpreting tongues was simply aping a heathen religious custom. But interpretation is from God.

Interpretation is the word used for interpreting from one language to another, as in:

'*Joseph spoke to his brother by an interpreter –* '[17]

When a tongues message is interpreted, it is as effective as a prophecy,[18] but tongues messages should not be brought in a meeting if there is not an interpreter present.[19]

I had a phone call one Sunday evening from a man who had recently become a Christian. He wanted to be filled with the Spirit and to have the initial sign of speaking in tongues. But he had a question he was stumbling over: 'Did interpretation mean that the interpreter was given divine understanding of the language so that he understood it just as an interpreter understands a foreign language?'

I explained that Spirit interpretation is not a word by word 'translation'. Instead, interpretation conveys the meaning of the tongues message. This explains why a lengthy tongues message may be interpreted in about half as many words, or a short message in tongues may have a lengthy interpretation.

Paul the Apostle advises the one who speaks in tongues to:

'*– pray that he may interpret –* '[20]

Interpretation is the other half of a useful duo of gifts which bring messages from God to the Church for its upbuilding.

A message in tongues must be interpreted, otherwise it is not understood.

But praying in tongues needs no interpretation. It is to God, not to men.

To the speaker in tongues, the difference between a message in tongues and prayer in tongues is as obvious as is the difference between preaching and praying to their speaker.

*'But all these worketh that one and the selfsame Spirit, dividing to every man severally as he will –'*

All these manifestations or gifts are effected, or accomplished, by the one Holy Spirit. This is a reminder of Who does these activities: not the Christian who is filled with the Spirit, but the Spirit Who fills the Christian.

And God divides or apportions the gifts. The word for 'divides' is used here and once again, in Luke 15 verse 12, where the father divided his goods so that the younger Prodigal Son could have his share.

This division is made to Christians as God decides; it is a choice by God. But a prerequisite is that the Christian be willing to let Him work through him in any way God chooses.

As an afterthought, may I just add that the Christian who phoned me on the Sunday evening with the problem over interpretation, was filled with the Spirit and received the sign of speaking in tongues later that evening. Hallelujah!

*Text references*
1. Proverbs 8 verse 11.
2. 1 John 4 verse 16.
3. 1 Corinthians 13 verses 1–13.
4. Romans 5 verse 5.
5. Luke 20 verses 23–25.
6. John 1 verses 47–50; John 2 verse 24; John 16 verse 30; John 21 verse 17.
7. Ephesians 2 verse 8.
8. Acts 12 verse 6.
9. Acts 5 verse 36.

10. Genesis 3 verse 15; Isaiah 53 verses 1f; Zechariah 11 verse 12; Acts 11 verses 27, 28; Acts 21 verses 10f.
11. Matthew 26 verses 67, 68; Luke 7 verse 39.
12. 2 Kings 5 verse 3.
13. Matthew 21 verses 26, 46.
14. Luke 7 verse 16.
15. 1 John 4 verses 1–3.
16. *The World Book Encyclopedia* (1974) Chicago: Field Vol. 12 page 62.
17. Genesis 42 verse 23.
18. 1 Corinthians 14 verse 5.
19. 1 Corinthians 14 verse 28.
20. 1 Corinthians 14 verse 13.

# CHAPTER EIGHT

# What are tongues for, anyway – ?

God has given the church the gift of tongues. It would be presumptuous of us to question His reasons for doing this, but since the Bible does tell us why, we really ought to know them.

There are five purposes for tongues.

## 1. A Sign

The first is that tongues is a sign. In the second chapter of Acts we read of Jews from surrounding nations who had gathered in Jerusalem during the Festival of Pentecost. They heard the disciples speak in tongues and were amazed for they heard their own languages:

' – the multitude – were confounded, because that every man heard them speak in his own language.'[1]

The multitude of Jews heard Galileans speak foreign languages they could not speak nor understand. On this occasion, tongues was a sign that something supernatural was taking place.

Tongues was also a sign that God had accepted the Gentile, Cornelius, along with those others who had gathered in his house to listen to Peter. When Peter had to justify the Jewish Believers in Jerusalem his going into the home of Cornelius, he said:

*'Forasmuch then as God gave them the like gift as he did unto us, who believed on the Lord Jesus Christ, what was I, that I could withstand God?'[2]*

*'When they (his fellow-believers in Jerusalem) heard these things, they held their peace, and glorified God, saying, Then hath God also to the Gentiles granted repentance unto life.'[3]*

What was the convincing evidence?

Peter and those Jewish Believers who accompanied him to the home of Cornelius:

*' – were astonished – because that on the Gentiles also was poured out the gift of the Holy Ghost.'[4]*

And how did they know the gift of the Holy Ghost had been poured out on Cornelius and his friends?

*'For they heard them speak with tongues, and magnify God.'[5]*

Peter and the other Jewish Believers would not have believed that Gentiles who were regarded as unclean, could be accepted by God, but the sign of speaking in tongues changed them from disbelief to belief.

In his letter to the church at Corinth, Paul said:

*'Wherefore tongues are for a sign, not to them that believe, but to them that believe not.'[6]*

Tongues is a sign to convince the doubter – the

unbeliever. The Jewish Believers had to be persuaded that Gentiles were accepted by God, and the out-pouring of the Holy Spirit on them and their speaking in tongues was the convincing evidence.

But the main effectiveness of tongues as a sign is to convince unbelievers – non-Christians. For it was the tongues of the disciples on the Day of Pentecost which caught the attention of the multitude, so that they listened to Peter, and of that multitude, three thousand believed and were baptised.[7]

## 2. *For magnifying God*
With a magnifying glass you see things bigger and clearer. What you see doesn't actually become bigger or clearer; but your perception is improved.

When we magnify God, we help improve people's perception of Him.

In the Cornelius experience of being filled with the Holy Spirit, we read that Peter heard the Gentiles speak with tongues and magnify God.[8] Speaking in tongues and magnifying God go together. One complements the other. Praise springs from tongues, and leads into worship. When we worship God, we acknowledge that He is God, and our worship is the proper response to what He is.

The relationship of tongues to praise and worship may be shown by this diagram:

*Speaking in Tongues*
makes you more aware of
the reality and goodness of ——→ 
God.

*Praise*
you want to thank Him for
His goodness, to extol Him,
both to His face, and before
others.

*Worship* ←
The goodness of God eventually
fills you with love and adoration
for Him. You may be at a loss
for words, or just repeat your love
for Him over and over again.

Praise and Worship does not depend on circumstances,
but on what you know of God. Speaking in tongues helps
the Christian to have a greater awareness of Him.

## 3. Tongues edifies the speaker

Paul says in his letter to the Corinthians:

'He that speaketh in an unknown tongue edifieth
himself—'[9]

That word 'edifieth' comes from the same word as
'edifice' or 'building', and it means 'to build up'. Speaking
in tongues builds up the Christian who speaks in tongues.
The Bible doesn't say specifically how the edifying
happens, but from my own experience and that of others,
the following points emerge:

(a) When you speak in tongues, you become more
aware of the nearness and reality of God. You have the
evidence of your own ears to prove that the Holy Spirit is
speaking through you. Your lips and tongue, teeth and
vocal chords, your breathing – they declare that God's
Spirit is speaking through you. This increases your faith.

(b) Speaking in tongues doesn't depend on how you feel, or on your circumstances, so that even in the depths of despair and gloom you may speak in tongues. Then you become aware of God operating in your circumstances.

(c) As shown already, tongues leads on to praise and worship, and these build up the Christian because they are part of a healthy relationship with God.

### 4. Tongues is speaking to God

The Bible says:

> 'For he that speaketh in an unknown tongues speaketh not unto men, but unto God—'[10]

And what does he say to God?

> '—in the spirit he speaketh mysteries—'[10]

That word 'mysteries' means the secret plans and purposes of God. Sometimes these 'mysteries' are revealed when the tongues are interpreted.

The Bible also says that praying in the spirit is praying in tongues.[11] Prayer is communication with God. But since tongues is one of the manifestations of the Holy Spirit, so prayer in tongues is a prayer of the Holy Spirit through the spirit of man, using his speech organs, a prayer to God the Father. This may be portrayed by this diagram:

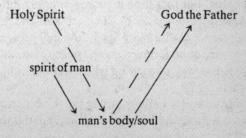

75

When we pray in tongues, our spirit[12] prays along with the Holy Spirit[13], a joint intercession. When a group of people pray 'The Lord's Prayer' together, that is a joint prayer.

So praying in tongues is a joint prayer – our spirit and God's Spirit in unison. We don't know what we are praying, but the Holy Spirit does – He directs it. And it is to God the Father.

This gives us the opportunity to be a co-worker with the Holy Spirit in doing God's will, because this prayer is 'according to the will of God.'[14]

Some years ago when I lived in Hong Kong, I was wakened from a deep sleep early one Monday morning. I had a great sense of urgency to pray for our oldest son, Paul, who was at university in Scotland. I didn't know what to pray for, but I felt led to pray in tongues, and so I did. After less than a minute, I stopped, lay back and slept. Next morning I told Jean about it.

A few days later, a letter arrived from Paul. He told us that before the evening service on the previous Sunday, a teenage Christian friend came to him in distress because he had been experimenting with praying to Satan. The friend said that a terrible black form had appeared before him and frightened him out of his wits.

As Paul was counselling him and praying, he felt an evil presence, so he cried out to God for protection. At that very moment, but in a time-zone seven hours different, I was wakened from my sleep. Then our son and his friend felt the presence of the Holy Spirit, the evil presence fled, and the friend found forgiveness and peace of mind.

Tongues is a way of praying when we don't know what to pray for.

Jean had a similar early-morning prayer experience as I had. Again it was early Monday morning, but this time the object of prayer was my oldest brother, Bill. Jean prayed for him in tongues, then slept, and next morning she told me about it.

A few days later, we learned that in the Sunday evening meeting, Bill and his wife, Jeannie, had both accepted Jesus as Lord and Saviour.

In both these instances, God stirred us up to pray in tongues, for loved ones thousands of miles away. We didn't know what to pray for, but we prayed in tongues, and God, Who 'is able to do exceeding abundantly above all that we ask or think, according to the power that worketh in us,'[15] worked the miracles. He chose to involve us supernaturally so that we could share in those blessings and spiritual struggles on the other side of the world.

## 5. Tongues brings messages from God

On its own, speaking in tongues helps only the speaker, apart from being a sign to unbelievers or doubters. Of course, since the speaker is part of the Church or Body of Christ, as he is edified, so to that extent is the Church edified. The manifestations of the Spirit – including tongues – are given to each man to profit by them.

But in addition to profiting the speaker, tongues when interpreted, also edify other Christians.[16] I have often heard interpretations of tongues which linked up well with prophecies given during the same meeting. The prophecies and tongues complemented each other.

*'I would that ye all spake with tongues, but rather that ye prophesied: for greater is he that prophesieth than he that speaketh with tongues, except he interpret, that the church may receive edifying.'*[16]

This agrees with the experience of the Ephesians who had never heard of the Holy Spirit, their baptism being John's Baptism. When Paul baptised them in the Name of Jesus Christ, they were filled with the Holy Spirit and spoke in tongues and prophesied.[17]

Tongues and prophecy go together, but because prophecy needs no interpretation, it is more useful than tongues. Tongues, however, is a gift from God, so we don't despise or forbid it – if we're wise.[18]

On many occasions I have heard tongues used along with other spiritual gifts – the gifts of healings, of words of knowledge and wisdom, of faith, discernment, prophecy and interpretation. Their close use with these and other gifts does not surprise me because it is the Holy Spirit Who does it all, and the use of tongues increases the faith of the speaker so that he is more open to the Holy Spirit to work through him. God has given speaking and praying in tongues for a purpose, and we must cherish them as from God, and use them to His glory.

*Text references*
1. Acts 2 verse 6.
2. Acts 11 verse 17.
3. Acts 11 verse 18.
4. Acts 10 verse 45.
5. Acts 10 verse 46.
6. 1 Corinthians 14 verse 22.
7. Acts 2 verse 41.
8. Acts 10 verse 46.
9. 1 Corinthians 14 verse 4.
10. 1 Corinthians 14 verse 2.
11. 1 Corinthians 14 verse 14.
12. 1 Corinthians 14 verse 14, 15.
13. Ephesians 6 verse 18.
14. Romans 8 verse 27.
15. Ephesians 3 verse 20.

16. 1 Corinthians 14 verse 5.
17. Acts 19 verse 6.
18. 1 Corinthians 14 verse 39.

# CHAPTER NINE

# Praise and Thanksgiving

Early one spring morning in 1983, I was praying. It was dark and dismal outside, but not so dark and dismal as I felt within my heart.

There were deep problems in my personal life, and as I began to pray for my children, I thought of our second son, Mark. He was a 'hippie', a university drop-out, living for his guitar and drugs. And on that March morning, I knew he was far from God and far from me. He was away from home and seldom wrote; we could only imagine how he was getting on.

Through my tears I prayed in tongues because I felt that the One Who could best pray for Mark is God. Then tongues gradually led me to praise God, then on to thanksgiving. And with my face still wet with tears, I laughed and rejoiced before God with my arms upraised as the dancing fire in the grate threw my shadow on the ceiling.

For me, tongues and praise go together, because when I hear God's Spirit praying through me, I feel His reality, and this leads to praise. Regardless of how I feel at the time.

But some Christians find it impossible to praise God if they are not happy. In fact, a minister once said to me that if he praised God when he didn't feel like doing it, he would be a hypocrite. For him, praise reflected his feelings. But I see praise as reflecting what God is, not my feelings.

If I say: 'My wife is a wonderful housekeeper, great at managing money, an excellent cook . . .' I am praising her, and these statements reflect truth which remains true regardless of how I feel at the time. Even if I did not say them, she would still be all these qualities. By praising her, I am voicing them.

Of course, it comes more easily to say them when things are going well, but if we've just disagreed over something and I'm feeling grumpy, she is still worthy of praise – she's still a wonderful person. It's just I don't feel like saying it.

So we praise God to say what He is, not how we feel.

The Bible uses various words for praise, and usually they indicate the feelings of the speaker – that he is feeling happy or wants to say something good about God.

But there is one word which has taught me a great deal about praise, for it tells me I should praise God even if I am unhappy, even if my earthly circumstances could not be worse.

We find it first in the story of Leah, the wife Jacob did not love; he preferred her sister, Rachel. Leah tried to win her husband's love by bearing him sons, and the names of the first three indicate this. But on the birth of her fourth son, she obviously decided it was a lost cause, so she shifted her attention to God and praised Him. She named her son, 'Praise' or 'Yadah' – or as we know it better: 'Judah'.[1]

'Yadah' does not really mean Praise, but rather 'to stretch out the hand' or 'to confess or witness to something' – rather like raising your hand to show whose side you are on.

Leah was unhappy at that time, yet she praised God.

In the same way, in Psalm 42, David poured out his unhappiness, yet twice in that Psalm, in verses 5 and 11, he said:

*'I shall yet praise (yadah) God.'*

Yadah is praise we do even when we don't feel like it.

In 2 Chronicles chapter 20, the Moabites and their allies invaded Judah, and King Jehoshaphat was in despair. But God commanded the army of Judah to stand still and He would fight for them. So Jehoshaphat gathered his people to praise (yadah) God in the sight of the enemy. When they did this, the Moabites and their allies attacked each other and the people of Judah stood and watched as the invading army destroyed itself.

It took faith to praise God in those circumstances, but that is the kind of faith which honours God, and the kind of faith which God honours.

Imagine an empty wagon standing underneath a grain silo – open the silo trap-door and the grain pours into the wagon. God desires to pour His blessing out upon us, and praising Him is one faith-way to open the trap-door.

One of the features of meetings of Spirit-filled Christians is that when they praise God, they often raise their hands above their heads. This is the stretched out hands of Yadah, and I've come to believe it is a spiritually instinctive way of praising God.

In chapter one I told you of the healing of Leung Sap and that she became a Christian. Let me give some more details.

On the Thursday afternoon after we heard she was healed and home from hospital, my wife and I took a young Chinese Salvationist, Alfred Chan, with us, when we called on her. We felt we needed him to interpret because whereas Jean's Cantonese could manage with a simple counselling and prayer for healing, more scriptural explanation was needed if Leung Sap wished to become a Christian.

We climbed the dark stairway to her home. On the landing we were admitted into a long room with many cubicles, each a home for a family.

When we entered, everyone stopped what they were doing to stare at us. In the communal cooking area at the far end, Leung Sap spotted us and oblivious to everyone else, she began calling, 'Praise the Lord! Praise the Lord!' as she hurried to welcome us, her hands raised high above her head.

The religions Leung Sap was familiar with were Buddhism and ancestor worship, so how did she know to worship God in this way? I believe it was her spiritual instinct guiding her in praise.

But Yadah is also an effort, an act of the will, as I'm sure it was for Leah, for David and for Jehoshaphat and the people of Judah in their tribulations. And that morning in March, 1983, it was an act of the will for me.

But tongues made it easy. Let me repeat what I said earlier: praying in tongues made God more real to me than my circumstances. In those circumstances, praising God became what my heart longed to do, even through tears.

It didn't stop there, however. For there was another aspect of that early morning experience.

Praise led on to thanksgiving.

I know God is good, loving and all-powerful. I know He is working in every circumstance and situation for the good of those who love Him and are called according to His purpose.[2] Therefore, by faith, I could thank Him for what He was going to do in Mark's life.

Doesn't the Bible say that:

'— *the mercy of the Lord is from everlasting to everlasting upon them that fear Him, and His righteousness unto children's children.'[3] . . ?*

His righteousness was unto my son Mark, towards all my children, and to my grandchildren. I really had something to thank God for.

What is more, because of my relationship with God through Jesus Christ, my son, all my children, are holy.[4] But let me hasten to add that the act of my being a Christian does not mean that my children are therefore Christians too. They have to make their own response to God. But they are in a relationship in which God regards them as His by right, and He will pursue them to become Christians.

Christian readers, our children belong to God, and we must have faith for them that when they come of age, they will acknowledge this and accept Jesus as their Saviour and Lord.

Praying in tongues helped me that March morning to remember this and to praise God and thank Him for what I believed He would do in Mark's life.

Now let me encourage you to thank God for your children, even your wayward ones. To thank God for all your circumstances – even those which are too terrible for words.

Firstly, the Bible says you should be:

*'Giving thanks always for all things unto God and the Father in the name of the Lord Jesus Christ:'[5] and again, 'In every thing give thanks; for this is the will of God in Christ Jesus concerning you.'[6]*

Thanks for *all* things? Yes! This is the will of God.
But how?
In the first text, the secret is in the word: 'for'. It is from

a Greek word which means doing something on behalf of, or for, another. It conjures up the picture of a soldier standing over a wounded friend, defending him.

Your thanksgiving stands *over* your circumstances. It is a statement of your faith that God is in your situation, and this kind of faith opens the trap-door of the silo to let God's grace and blessing fall upon you.

And your thanksgiving is *in* or *in the midst* of your circumstances, an act of faith like yeast in a lump of dough. Thanksgiving injects faith into the most hopeless predicament, and permits God's grace and power to work in it.

So give thanks 'for' and 'in' everything. And that is what I was doing that dark spring morning in 1983.

Later that same day, about 10.30 p.m., I returned home after a prayer meeting. Jean was at the ironing-board; our youngest son, Andrew, was in bed. But my wife wasn't ironing. She was on the phone. Turning to me as I entered the room, she offered me the receiver, saying: 'It's Mark.'

I was delighted because we so seldom heard from him, and usually it was just a scrap of news. 'Thank you, Lord,' I thought . . .


. . . and Mark's first words to we were: 'Hello, brother in Christ.'


For he had found Jesus as his Saviour and Lord.

That morning, heartbroken and despairing, I had reached out to God praying in the Spirit, and tongues had lifted me to praise and thanksgiving and joy.

Now, at the close of that same day, my praise and thanksgiving and joy overlept the confines of my language, and I found release in tongues . . .

*Text references*

1. Genesis 29 verses 31–35.
2. Romans 8 verse 28.
3. Psalm 103 verse 17.
4. 1 Corinthians 7 verse 14.
5. Ephesians 5 verse 20.
6. 1 Thessalonians 5 verse 18.

# CHAPTER TEN

# Down-to-earth Mystics

In the Saturday Sermon of a local newspaper, a minister wrote that while mystics might have direct access to God, most of us are not mystics, and that direct access to God is not the way for us.

I don't know whom his 'most of us' referred to, but it can hardly have been Christians. For we Christians do have direct access to God – and Jesus made it possible.

The bible is a record of people who had a relationship with God. And not only the 'spiritual giants' – the household names – but the 'all flesh' – the sons and daughters, young men, old men, servants and handmaids of Joel chapter 2 and Acts chapter 2. In the Bible, ordinary everyday people had direct access to God.

The Concise Oxford Dictionary defines a mystic as:

'One who seeks by contemplation and self-surrender to obtain union with or absorption into the Deity, or who believes in spiritual apprehension of truths beyond the understanding.'

Was Paul praying for the handful of mystics, the few outstanding Christians, when he prayed:

'– that ye – may be able to comprehend with all saints what

*is the breadth, and length, and depth, and height, and to
know the love of Christ which passeth knowledge, that ye
might be filled with all the fulness of God –* '[1]

Or was he praying for all Christians? The first verse of
Ephesians, the one which contains the address, clearly
says:

' *– to the saints which are at Ephesus, and to the faithful
in Christ Jesus.'*

If you love the Lord, if you are a Christian, you come into
that second category – 'the faithful in Christ Jesus'. So let
us look at what Paul prayed for us. We'll examine some of
the words in the prayer.

'comprehend' – it really means 'to lay hold of so as to
make one's own'.[2] That is no 'airy-fairy' experience, but a
real-life encounter with the love of Christ.

'and to know' – The Christian is to know the love of
Christ. But not as a theory picked up second-hand from
some other more spiritual Christian, but by personal
experience.

The other week I was told of a man who went for an
interview for a position with a Christian association, and
after saying all the correct things to the selection committee
and apparently making the right responses, was surprised
to be turned down. The Chairman went on to tell him: 'Mr
X, you certainly know all that you need to know, but you
seem to have learned it all from other people.'

There are four root-words translated 'know' in the New
Testament, and the word used in this passage means – 'a
knowledge grounded in personal experience.'[2]

The Christian is to have a personal experience of God,
one which is real, not theoretical. It is an experience by

88

faith, an experience of stepping out in the dark and finding the rock beneath his feet.

*'If we live in the Spirit, let us also walk in the Spirit.'*[3]

That 'walk in the Spirit' means to let ourselves exhibit the control of the Spirit in our lives. If that has to be called mystical, so be it, but that experience is God's will for all Christians. We are expected to have such a relationship with God by the indwelling Spirit that our lives are in harmony with Him. His will should be lived out in us. His power revealed in us.

Ian Gowans is a joiner. Anyone less like the conventional 'mystic' you could hardly find. But Ian is also a Spirit-filled Christian. Late one Saturday evening, God told him to visit a local minister because the minister was 'in a spot of bother'. Ian had no idea what the bother might be, but off he went. The minister was surprised to see him, but since they knew each other as Christians, Ian found the courage to tell him what God had told him to do.

'Well, I have a problem,' agreed the minister, 'because something has gone wrong with the car and I can't get it to start. I need it first thing in the morning and the garages are closed. A mechanic had a look at it tonight but he can't find the fault.'

Without looking at the car, Ian suddenly knew what was wrong.

'God says you've not to worry. Everything'll be all right. It's a blockage in the carburettor – a dirty jet.'

Ian had no idea where the knowledge came from, but he spoke it out to the glory of God.

Next morning, the mechanic came early, and found it was just as Ian had said. And the minister fulfilled his duties on time.

Was that the mystical experience of the few, or an ordinary Christian so yielded to the Holy Spirit's influence that God can use him just as He will? That's what being filled with the Holy Spirit and manifesting His gifts is all about, for what Ian had displayed was the gift of knowledge.

The dictionary definition of a mystic reminds me of two more verses from the Bible:

*'I beseech you therefore, brethren, by the mercies of God, that ye present your bodies a living sacrifice, holy, acceptable unto God – and be ye transformed.'*[4]

and the next one:

*'The things of God knoweth no man, but the Spirit of God. Now we have received – the Spirit which is of God – that we might know the things that are freely given to us of God.'*[5]

According to that, every Christian is to be a mystic.

But it is better to seek instead the experience described in Galatians 2 verse 20:

*'I am crucified with Christ, nevertheless I live, yet not I, but Christ liveth in me: and the life which I now live in the flesh I live by the faith of the Son of God, who loved me and gave himself for me.'*

That should be the goal of every Christian.

In every man there are two forces which are in tension, pulling one against the other.

One is the need to explain and control his environment. This gives rise to scientific thought, and is basically, behind the rejection of the supernatural, even by Christians.

The other is the necessity to come to terms with the big

mysteries of life: where I came from, why I'm here, where I am going. And religion is our response to that.

Christians must hold these forces in balance. And Spirit-filled Christians are equipped to do it.

*Text references*
1. Ephesians 3 verses 18, 19.
2. Thayer – ibid.
3. Galatians 5 verse 25.
4. Romans 12 verses 1, 2.
5. 1 Corinthians 2 verses 11, 12.

# CHAPTER ELEVEN

# ' – tongues shall cease . . .'

One Sunday afternoon, the doorbell rang. I answered it and there was a Brethren evangelist who was visiting the houses in the district with tracts. I know him as a hard-working servant of the Lord who is tireless in preaching the Gospel to young and old alike.

We talked for a few minutes, and he wanted to know what I believed – where I stood in the Christian faith. So the experience of being filled with the Holy Spirit came up and I told him what I know about the gifts of the Spirit.

'But tongues aren't for today,' he insisted, 'they were for the setting-up of the Church. Now that the perfect is come we don't need them.'

'What do you mean by – "the perfect is come"?' I queried.

'The Bible,' he replied. 'The Bible is the perfect revelation from God – so there's no need now for imperfect revelation. That's what tongues are – imperfect ways of getting messages from God.'

He was referring to a passage in 1 Corinthians chapter 13:

*'Charity never faileth: but whether there be prophecies, they shall fail; whether there be tongues, they shall cease; whether there be knowledge, it shall vanish away. For we*

*know in part, and we prophesy in part. But when that which is perfect is come, then that which is in part shall be done away. When I was a child, I spake as a child, I understand as a child, I thought as a child: but when I became a man I put away childish things. For now we see through a glass, darkly; but then face to face: now I know in part; but then shall I know even as also I am known.*[1]

This chapter tells us how important love is; it lasts for eternity – it shall never cease. But prophecies, tongues and knowledge – they will pass away when the perfect is come.

Since prophecy and tongues are supernatural ways by which God gives knowledge to His servants, we may assume that the knowledge referred to in verse 8 of the same passage is the gift of knowledge.[2] What the chapter is saying then, is that gifts which reveal knowledge or messages from God, will cease when the perfect knowledge is come.

The Brethren evangelist who came to my door said the perfect knowledge had already come. But was he right. Let us examine the passage.

Verse 9 refers to the inadequacy of knowledge and prophecy, and verse 10 to their being replaced when the perfect is come. Tongues are not specifically referred to as being replaced, but verse 11 refers to the speech of the child being superseded by adult things in adulthood. So when shall these inadequate gifts be superseded, when shall childish things be done away?

Verse 12 tells us: when we see face to face, and we know as we are known. In this life, we never see the Lord in that way, we never know as we are known. We have to live by faith.[3] Even the use of the gifts of the Spirit is an exercise of faith.

Perfect face-to-face knowledge, knowing God as we are known – that is not yet. Perfection is yet to come; we await it.[4] Now we see as through a glass darkly.[5] But that is how it should be, for without faith it is impossible to please God.[6] When we no longer have blinkers over our spiritual eyes, we no longer see God and His truth as 'through a glass darkly' – but as face to face – then shall tongues and prophecy and the gift of knowledge cease.

Another argument that tongues have ceased is in comparing the list of the gifts of the Spirit in 1 Corinthians chapter 12 with that in Ephesians chapter 4 verse 11. The Ephesian list does not include tongues, and since the letter to Corinth was to correct a faulty church, while the one to Ephesus was to a more spiritual church – as some would claim – the implication is that the more spiritual you are, the less likely you are to speak in tongues. Or, since it is believed that the letter to the Corinthians was written earlier than the one to the Ephesians, that while tongues was still being used in Corinth, by the time Paul had written to the Ephesians, tongues had ceased.

Here are the two lists:

| *Corinthians* | *Ephesians* |
| --- | --- |
| the word of wisdom | apostles |
| the word of knowledge | prophets |
| faith | evangelists |
| gifts of healing | pastors |
| working of miracles | teachers |
| prophecy | |
| discerning of spirits | |
| divers kinds of tongues | |
| interpretation of tongues | |

When we place the two lists together, we see a fundamental difference between them: the Ephesian list is of offices or positions in the church; while the Corinthian list is of abilities or manifestations of the Spirit through Christians, both office-bearers and lay people.

A less obvious difference between them is that two different words for 'gifts' are used in the two passages. In Ephesians, it is 'doma' which is linked with a verb and emphasises the act of giving, while in Corinthians, it is 'charisma' which speaks of grace or favour conferred on one.

The fact that Paul uses two different words for these gifts given by God surely indicate that in his thinking they were different kinds of gifts.

Faith is not mentioned in the Ephesian list, but surely no one would say that the gift of faith had ceased. Therefore we cannot say that tongues had ceased just because it also is not in the Ephesian list.

Does the Bible say that tongues were to continue after the early days of the New Testament church?

Most Christian scholars agree that the Mark 16 verses 9 to 20 passage is not in the two earliest manuscripts we have, so the reference in verse 17 to speaking in tongues is not a proof for speaking in tongues today. But if we accept that, we are left with the conclusion that someone, or perhaps a church, in the days immediately following the days of the Apostles, thought that speaking in tongues was important enough to add these verses on to Mark's Gospel. And for an error to have been preserved by at least part of the church, a part important enough for its translation to have found its way into our Bibles, suggests that for some time after the New Testament church at least, speaking in tongues was being used.

Nothing in the Acts of the Apostles suggests that

tongues were a temporary phenomenon. In the story of Cornelius and his friends becoming Christians, there is no doubt that speaking in tongues was the proof that the gift of the Holy Spirit had been given to them.

*' – on the Gentiles also was poured our the gift of the Holy Ghost. For they heard them speak with tongues, and magnify God –'*[7]

Those who disagree with the 'charismatic' view, say that this was a sign for the one occasion, to show that Gentiles may become followers of Jesus Christ, an inaugural sign, similar to the occasion of the Day of Pentecost, when Jews became for the first time members of the Body of Christ. On these two occasions, tongues were a sign, they say, not simply that they had received the infilling of the Holy Ghost, but that they had been admitted into what is now known as the Church.

But there is evidence that speaking in tongues accompanied the infilling of the Holy Spirit on other occasions. For example, the Samaritans who were filled with the Spirit:

*'Then they laid their hands on them (the Samaritans), and they received the Holy Ghost. And when Simon saw that through laying on of the apostles' hands the Holy Ghost was given –'*[8]

Simon saw that the Holy Ghost was given. The word 'saw' means in Greek – 'to learn by looking'[16] There was obviously some external sign or indication that the Holy Spirit was given. The only sign common to the Pentecostal outpouring and the Cornelius experience, was speaking in tongues. It is true that you hear tongues, but when people speak in tongues, you can also see something happening.

When Paul came to Ephesus on one occasion, he found twelve disciples who had received John's baptism. They were then baptised in the name of Jesus, and:

> ' – when Paul had laid his hands upon them, the Holy Ghost came on them; and they spake with tongues, and prophesied.'[9]

I've heard it said by those opposed to charismatic gifts that this was also an inaugural sign – a special sign to people who had received John's baptism that they could be received by Jesus Christ and have the gift of the Holy Spirit.[10] But it is most likely that some of Jesus' disciples had also been baptised by John the Baptist as Jesus Himself had been.[11] Almost certainly, Andrew the brother of Peter, had received John's baptism.

Speaking in tongues is mentioned eighteen times in 1 Corinthians.[12] The one verse which mentions tongues ceasing is in chapter 13 verse 8, and it has already been explained.

We are told to desire spiritual gifts, especially prophecy,[13] and not to forbid speaking in tongues.[14] That doesn't suggest that Paul saw tongues as temporary. On the contrary, he wrote this letter to instruct Believers as how to use tongues correctly.

> 'How is it then, brethren? When ye come together, every one of you hath a psalm, hath a doctrine, hath a tongue, hath a revelation, hath an interpretation. Let all things be done unto edifying. If any man speak in an unknown tongue, let it be by two, or at the most by three, and that by course; and let one interpret. But if there be no

*interpreter, let him keep silence in the church; and let him speak to himself, and to God.'*[15]

Paul clearly makes a place in the worship of the church for speaking in tongues. No one can read that and say that speaking in tongues was just a sign to prove that Jew and Gentile may receive the gift of the Holy Spirit, and that after the first inaugural outpouring, there was no need for any more Jews or Gentiles to speak in tongues; tongues were an ongoing happening in the church, even to having two or three messages in a service.

That advice for the Christian to 'speak to himself and to God' is advice I often follow when I am in a church which doesn't have tongues in its tradition. I can pray in tongues within myself throughout a minister's sermon as support for him, while my rational understanding listens to his words.

An interesting text on the subject of the continuation of tongues, and of all the gifts of the Holy Spirit, is 1 Corinthians 1 verse 7:

*'So that ye come behind in no gift; waiting for the coming of our Lord, Jesus Christ.'*

The word 'coming' is the Greek word 'apokalupsis' which means 'unveiling' and is used here referring to the coming again of Jesus in glory. Paul says that he thanks God that these Corinthians are enriched by Christ, and that they come behind in no gift as they wait the return in glory of Jesus Christ.

What does that phrase 'come behind in no gift' mean?

The word for gift is 'charisma' – the same word for 'gift' as in 'gifts of the Spirit'.

To 'come behind' is 'to fall behind, to lack, to fail to be

98

a partaker, to be devoid of, to suffer want'.[16] And Paul thanks God that they lack no gift of the Spirit as they await the return of Jesus Christ.

Christian churches should ask themselves:

'Would Paul thank God that we are enriched in everything, and do not lack any of the gifts of the Spirit as we await the return of the Lord Jesus Christ?'

We must remember that these gifts are 'manifestations' of the Holy Spirit. It is dangerous to say that the Holy Spirit no longer works in the church as He did in New Testament times. Before anyone makes such a drastic claim – with its implication that the gifts in the church today are not of the Holy Spirit – he must have definite proof from the Bible. And there is none.

On the contrary, the weight of Biblical evidence supports the experience of Christians down the centuries, and in increasing numbers as the return of the Lord Jesus Christ draws nearer: that the Holy Spirit still manifests Himself.

Finally, prejudice is not evidence. It is safer for the Christian who is against tongues to say he does not know, and to keep an open mind. Then he is more likely to find the truth: that the infilling of the Holy Spirit and His gifts are still with us.

*Text references*
1. 1 Corinthians 13 verses 8–12.
2. 1 Corinthians 13 verse 8.
3. Galatians 3 verse 11.
4. Romans 8 verses 18–25.
5. 1 Corinthians 13 verse 12.
6. Hebrews 11 verse 6.

7. Acts 10 verses 45, 46.
8. Acts 8 verses 17, 18.
9. Acts 19 verse 6.
10. Acts 19 verses 1–7.
11. John 1 verses 35–40.
12. Chapter 12 verses 10, 28, 30; Chapter 13 verses 8 and possibly verse 1; Chapter 14 verses, 2, 4, 5, 6, 13, 14, 16, 18, 19, 22, 23, 26, 27, 39
13. 1 Corinthians 14 verse 1.
14. 1 Corinthians 14 verse 39.
15. 1 Corinthians 14 verses 26–28.
16. Thayer, J. H. (1976) *'Greek–English Lexicon'*

# CHAPTER TWELVE

# Down through History

If tongues are to continue until 'that which is perfect is come', until we see 'face to face', and 'know even as also I am known', if they are not to cease until they are replaced by the perfect knowledge of the presence of the glorified Lord – if that is so – then why don't we hear of tongues in the history of the Church? It seems to be only in this century that Christians experience the gifts of the Spirit.

What did happen to speaking in tongues? There seems to be centuries of silence.

One thing we do know is that in by-gone days, people who spoke in tongues could be charged with witchcraft or blasphemy. An example of this from the 18th century was Mother Ann Lee of the Shakers, an offshoot of the Quakers, who was accused of blasphemy because she said she could speak in tongues as the Apostles did.[1]

And another reason may have been that those who did speak in tongues kept it secret, or were unimportant people so that history did not record them.

One of the Early Church leaders, named Irenaeus, writing about 185 AD, said:

'In like manner do we also hear (or have heard) many brethren in the Church who possess prophetic gifts, and who through the Spirit speak all kinds of tongues, and bring to light for the common benefit the hidden things of men and declare the mysteries of God, whom also the apostle terms spiritual – '[2]

At the beginning of the next century, another church leader, Tertullian was having a dispute with an opponent named Marcion who was teaching heretical beliefs. Tertullian challenged Marcion to produce from among his followers, as Tertullian could from among his:

'– prophets such as have spoken not by human sense, but with the Spirit of God, such as have predicted things to come – by the Spirit, in an ecstasy, that is – whenever an interpretation of tongues has occurred to him – '[3]

If there were interpretations of tongues, then there must have been the tongues to interpret.

Speaking in tongues were recorded as taking place in the Waldensian church in the 11th century. The Waldensian church was confined at that time to the north of Italy. Its members were determined to live according to the Bible and were eventually excommunicated from the Roman Catholic church. One belief is that this church was founded in the 11th century, but another is that it traces its existence back to the missionary work of Paul in Italy. Its headquarters today is in Rome.

Another church with the gift of tongues was the Camisards – a Protestant church of the Cevennes, France – in the 17th century. To quote from Hastings' 'Encyclopedia', those Camisards –

'spoke with tongues – quite uneducated persons gave utterances when 'seized by the Spirit', to prophecies, in the purest French –'

Members of the early Methodist Church may also have spoken in tongues. A reference in the diary of a methodist, one Thomas Walsh, for March 8th, 1740, is believed to refer to his receiving the gift of tongues:

'This morning, the Lord gave me language that I knew not of, raising my soul to Him in a wonderful manner – '[4]

In 1820, a wonderful event happened in the West of Scotland. An invalid girl, Mary Campbell, was in bed studying the Bible when she reached an important conclusion:[5]

' – if Jesus as a man in my nature thus spake and thus performed mighty works by the Holy Ghost, which he even promiseth me, then ought I in the same Spirit to do likewise the works which he did and greater works than these – '

' – having thus argued with herself, Mary Campbell first began to speak in tongues and then rose from her bed healed.'

But even if examples of speaking in tongues could be found for each of the last twenty centuries – and many can be – it still would not change one fact: that speaking in tongues had almost ceased to exist for long centuries between the days of the Early Church and this century.

It is encouraging to see, however, that when the gifts of the Spirit did occur, it was usually among groups of Christians who were struggling against the formalism of the established church and against unscriptural doctrines and practices – among groups who were having Spiritual revival or renewal, such as during the Great Awakening in

103

America, and in the revivals in Scotland and Wales.[6]

Is there a reason why the gifts of the Spirit almost died out during those centuries?

If we look at early church worship, we see that there were both fixed order of service or liturgy – and free spiritual utterances.[7] The Apostle Paul gave instructions on how this should be done.[8] But in order for this to be effective, there had to be self-discipline as well as discipline imposed by church leaders. They had to be able to judge between an utterance which was from God's Spirit, and one which was of the speaker only.

A lay member of the church could still bring a prophecy, or a message in tongues with interpretation. And under ideal conditions, this was a good thing. It could lead, however, to indiscipline and heresy if spiritual authority and discernment were lacking.

About this time, freedom of spiritual utterance became less common in the church and more emphasis was given to a formal liturgy.

A clue to this change may be found in the writing of Justin Martyr who lived in the middle of the second century. On the one hand he could say:

'It is possible to see amongst us women and men who possess the gifts of the Spirit of God – '[9]

referring, apparently, to the gifts as they are listed in 1 Corinthians chapter 12. But he has this to say about the order of service of worship:

'On the day called after the sun a meeting – takes place – and the Memoirs of the Apostles or the writings of the Prophets are read – the leader delivers an address – then we all rise and send heavenwards prayers – bread and wine mixed with water are laid down – the people join in, in saying the 'Amen'; and now comes the distribution to each and the common meal – '[10]

Justin spoke about the gifts of the Spirit, yet he didn't mention them in the order of service although the Apostle Paul gave instructions for their use. It may be, however, that the reference to them all standing and sending 'heavenwards prayers' is united praying in tongues which occurs in Pentecostalist and Charismatic groups today.

So a possible reason for the disappearance of speaking in tongues from the church may be that it was thought to be a threat to order and discipline. But behind it all, Satan plays on the conflict between man's desire to worship God perfectly and his basic insecurity and lack of confidence that God can make all things work for good.[11]

Eventually, the gifts of the Spirit appeared in the church again. On 1st January, 1901, the Holy Spirit fell upon students in a Bible college in Topeka, Kansas, and thus began the modern Pentecostal movement. Speaking in tongues and other gifts of the Spirit became widespread in the twentieth century, but because of opposition from existing churches, those who received the gifts had to band together to form separate churches, and so were formed the Elim Church, the Pentecostal and Apostolic churches, the Assemblies of God, and so on.

Then in the second half of this century, the Holy Spirit broke into established churches, but this time those who received these Spiritual gifts were able to stay on in their churches, with some exceptions, and so we have Church Renewal or Charismatic Movements in many churches today, including the Episcopal, the Anglican, the Roman Catholic and Presbyterian. Recently, the Baptist Church in Scotland produced a policy document which allows for the existence of charismatic ministers and groups within their fellowship.

*The Latter Rain Theory*

A scriptural prophecy which throws light on the dearth of Holy Spirit gifts or manifestations in the Church beween the second and twentieth centuries, is found in Joel chapter 2 verse 23:

*'Be glad then, you children of Zion, and rejoice in the Lord your God: for He gives you the former or early rain in just measure and in righteousness, and He causes to come down for you the rain, the former rain and the latter rain, as before.' (Amp.)*

The prophecy refers to the land of Israel being restored after it had been destroyed by a plague of locusts. But since verse 20 shows that the locusts are symbolic of the northern army and points to 'the final day of the Lord', when 'my People shall never be put to shame', (verses 26, 27), we have to see the promise of the former and the latter rains as meaning something else on a larger time-scale.

In verses 28 to 32 of that chapter, Joel prophesies both about the Day of Pentecost in Acts chapter 2, and to a future Day of the Lord: a split-level prophecy.

In this context, the *Latter Rain Theory* treats verse 23 as a split-level prophecy.

The former rain is seen as the outpouring of the Holy Spirit on the New Testament church. The latter rain means the outpouring of the Spirit since 1st January, 1901. In speaking of the former rain, Joel was thinking of the rain which fell in the Autumn when the seed had first been sown. This rain helped the seed to germinate. Then came the winter time from November to March, when it was cold and mostly dry with only very occasional light showers.

In the spring came the latter rains. These were heavy warm showers and they helped to swell the grain in the ears, just before the harvest. You can see why such a prophecy is attractive, especially since it comes only a few verses before the prophecy of the Holy Spirit coming upon all flesh, which Peter used as an explanation of what was happening on the Day of Pentecost. [12]

But are we permitted to think of the 'former rain and the latter rain' as referring to the Holy Spirit? The prophet Hosea, who lived about the same time as Joel, gave this prophecy:

' – the Lord: his going forth is prepared as the morning; and he shall come unto us as the rain, as the latter and former rain unto the earth.' [13]

So we see that in the days of Joel, the term 'former rain and latter rain' could refer to the Lord or His Spirit.

There are many references in the Bible to the Spirit being poured out upon men, [14] so we may justifiably speak of the 'former rain and the latter rain' as referring to two outpourings of the Spirit.

The spiritual drought implied by the Latter Rain Theory is challenged by some who ask:

'Are you saying that the Christians of all those non-charismatic centuries were not filled with the Holy Spirit – they were not so open to God – were not so filled with faith – as Pentecostalists and Charismatics today?'

To which one must reply: No matter how loving or faithful a Christian is, if he has received the infilling of the Holy Spirit and yet, for whatever reason, does not allow the Holy Spirit to manifest Himself through him, then the supernatural gifts will not be seen in his life. We must willingly co-operate with the Spirit.

I was asked to lead a charismatic meeting in Hong Kong when its leaders were on homeland furlough. At the end of one of the meetings, a missionary-wife and mother of three daughters, asked for prayer because her doctor had told her that afternoon, that her womb had collapsed and her five-months pregnancy was going to miscarry.

She was very distressed and tearful as a few of us gathered round and laid hands on her. We all prayed – all except myself. I remember that my wife, Jean, prayed specifically for the womb to return to its proper position.

But I couldn't pray, because I was having a struggle about obeying God. He was telling me to prophesy – to tell her that she would have a good pregnancy and that her baby – 'he' – would be born safely in the fulness of time. I didn't want to speak because at any time in the next few months I could be proved a false prophet.

Then God asked me if my main concern was to obey Him, or not to look foolish. I apologised, and I spoke the prophecy. In the fulness of her time, to the very day, after her womb had gone back to its proper position, she gave birth to a son.

If that young woman had lived in an age when prophecy and tongues were regarded as blasphemy, when healing was witchcraft – we who gathered round and laid hands on her that evening and prayed and prophesied – we would have remained silent about it – or perhaps, not even done this thing which God asked of us.

For one reason or another, the Church has struggled along for centuries without the gifts of the Spirit. But that is no reason for us to refuse God's power today.

*Text references*

1. Quoted in Cutten, G. B. (1927) *Speaking with Tongues* New Haven: YUP.
2. Hastings, J. (1932) *Encyclopedia of Religion and Ethics* Edinburgh: Clark.
3. Hastings – ibid.
4. Walsh's Diary, March 8, 1740.
5. Irving, E. (1832) *Facts connected with recent Manifestations of Spiritual Gifts* – quoted in Smail, T. A. (1975) *Reflected Glory* London: Hodder.
6. Hoekema, A. A. (1976) *What about Tongue Speaking* Exeter: Paternoster.
7. Cullman, O. (1953) *Early Christian Worship* London, S.C.M.
8. 1 Corinthians 14 verses 26–31.
9. *Ante-Nicene Fathers* Amer. Edn. Vol. 1.
10. Cullman, O. – ibid.
11. John 4 verse 23; Romans 8 verse 28.
12. Acts 2 verses 16, 21.
13. Hosea 6 verse 3.
14. Isaiah 32 verse 15; Ezekiel 39 verse 29; Joel 2 verse 28; Zechariah 12 verse 10.

## CHAPTER THIRTEEN

# What is 'Praying in the Spirit'?

As far as I was concerned, praying in the Spirit and praying in tongues were one and the same.

'Not so,' disagreed a friend. 'Praying in the Spirit is when you pray in your own language, but you're inspired by the Holy Spirit.'

That clash of opinions was at the back of my mind when I first wrote this chapter. I was determined to justify my point of view. And in the original draft of this chapter, I did just that . . . at least to my own satisfaction. Well, perhaps not quite – for there remained a niggling doubt.

My conscience bothered me, for I know we should never study the Bible just to prove a point, but to hear what God wants to say to us.

So I tore up the chapter and laid myself open to the Lord. 'All right, Lord, here I am . . . teach me.'

I discovered a great sense of relief when I abandoned my prejudices and opened my mind to whatever God wanted to teach me from His word. And after weeks of prayer and reading and meditation and waiting before the Lord, what He showed me quite simply, was this:

'When I pray in tongues, I am praying in the Spirit – yet there may be times when I pray in my own language and still be praying in the Spirit.'

That may not be a new revelation for you, but it was to me at the time, because it meant I had to readjust my ideas.

How did it come about?

My first step had been to compile a list of texts and passages from the Bible which had some bearing on the subject. You'll find that list at the end of this chapter.

Then I asked myself:

'What is this praying in the Spirit which is mentioned in both Ephesians and Jude?'[22,23]

I looked up both these texts and found that the term 'in the Spirit' is a translation of the Greek phrase: 'en pneuma'.

Now 'en pneuma' is a technical term. It is used in the Bible to describe when a person is so influenced by the Holy Spirit that he does or says things he could not if he were moved only by his own ability. Examples of this 'in the Spirit' behaviour are:

when the old man in the Temple, Simeon, was given supernatural knowledge to recognise the Christ Child as He whom Israel had been waiting for;[7]

or for Jesus, after His baptism, being led 'in the Spirit' into the wilderness;[8]

and John, the writer of the Book of Revelation, being 'in the Spirit' on various occasions.[9,10,11,12]

So praying 'in the Spirit' is being so inspired by the Holy Spirit that the prayer surpasses anything one could do in one's own capacity.

To digress for a moment: it's been said that the 'walking in the Spirit' references in Galatians[24] are also this kind of 'in the Spirit' experience. But that is only partially correct. In Galatians, 'walking in the Spirit' is not 'en pneuma', and is more correctly translated: 'by the Spirit'.

So to continue . . .

Praying in the Spirit refers to prayer in the power of the Holy Spirit – prayer which is more than the individual is able to do on his own.

The next question I wanted an answer for was:

'Is the praying in the spirit in 1 Corinthians[16] the same as the praying in the Spirit in Ephesians and Jude?'

In all three references, the words 'praying' and 'spirit' are the same. But there is an important difference. In Corinthians, it is 'toe pneumati', while in the other two references, it is 'en pneumati'. And while 'toe' may mean 'in the', it is more likely to mean 'with the' or 'by the'.

So what does this difference mean?

In the Corinthian passage, Paul says –

' – if I pray in an unknown tongue, my spirit prayeth – '[16]

That shows very clearly that praying in tongues is praying with the human spirit. But we already know that tongues is a manifestation of the Holy Spirit.[13] Therefore, it must be a joint activity of the human spirit and the Holy Spirit. An example of this kind of working together is:

' – the Spirit itself beareth witness with our spirit, that we are the children of God.'[4]

It's interesting to note that the term for 'bear witness' is used of two people putting their names as joing signatories to a document.

The Holy Spirit's involvement in praying in tongues may be seen in:

' – *the Spirit itself maketh intercession for us with groanings which cannot be uttered –* '[5]

We may speculate that praying in tongues is our tapping into this Holy Spirit intercession, but without definite proof, we should not pursue it too far.

However, since praying with the human spirit and praying in the Holy Spirit both refer to basically the same activity, why should there be a different expression in 1 Corinthians, when the 'en pneumati' of Ephesians and Jude would have done as well?

The answer is that in Corinthians, man's self-discipline and his control over tongues is emphasised. In Ephesians, God's help against spiritual enemies is the theme, so it is His Spirit Who is referred to. In Jude, those having not the Spirit of God are contrasted with those who have; again, the Holy Spirit is emphasised.

Now, what I had not believed was that praying in the Spirit could be praying in a language known to the speaker. But now I saw that this is so, though there is no text in the Bible which specifically says so. What changed my mind then?

It was when I discovered in Matthew's Gospel the words of Jesus:

'*How then doth David in the Spirit (en pneuma) call him Lord, saying, The Lord said to my Lord –* '[6]

Here was David, using his own language, speaking 'en pneuma'. And if he could speak 'in the Spirit', it must therefore be possible for us to pray 'in the Spirit' while

113

using our own language.

God is sovereign. He can do whatever He wants. And if He wishes someone to pray in English 'in the Spirit', then so be it.

There is one notable factor in favour of praying in tongues, however. When I pray in tongues, I know that both my spirit and God's Spirit are working together in it. I know I am obeying the command to 'pray in the Spirit'.

But when I pray in English, well – looking back over some thirty years of Christian experience, I recall only a few times when I believe I was praying in the Spirit. That's a personal notion, however, and there may be many who feel that they often pray in their own language and in the Spirit at the same time.

For me, the only time I know for certain I am praying in the Spirit is when I pray in tongues. And again, speaking personally, I find this helpful and encouraging.

Let me share with you what I was told recently in a letter from a young man not long after he was filled with the Holy Spirit. He says:

'I was sitting on some swings (in a city park) yesterday, when some 'boot-boys' came and started messin' up the swings along from me. They looked my age, but were probably younger; they were big and hard-looking anyway. Even when I first saw them approaching I began to feel frightened – funnily enough, it took, 'Ha! Where's your faith in God now?' to actually remind me, so I booted out the fear. After a while, while they were messin' up the swings, I decided to try prayin' in the Spirit, under my breath, turned away from them, with eyes shut. Impeccable timing. As I started, the swings stopped. I kept on praying and listened as they all decided to bop off! Wild!'

There you have an incident which could have been serious for that young Christian, but he obeyed the command in Ephesians and prayed in the Spirit by praying in tongues.

Before we close this chapter, let us look at a question which is a problem for some Christians: and that is – 'Should we all pray in tongues?' The Bible says that only some people speak in tongues which when they are interpreted, are messages from God.[13,14,15,19]

But on the day of Pentecost, and again in the home of Cornelius at Caesarea, everyone prayed and praised God in tongues, and there is no hint that their tongues were interpreted, nor that only certain individuals were supposed to use tongues.[1,2] And again, the command to 'pray in the Spirit' does not appear to be for only selected Christians, but for all the faithful in Christ Jesus.[25]

These uses of tongues are analogous to our using our own language. We don't all bring messages from God, in sermons or by prophecy or whatever: but we all have to pray. So while only some speak in tongues, everyone may pray in tongues. ·

Now, a final point . . .

'How do I know I'm praying when I use tongues?'

As a child in primary school in Scotland, each morning I had to stand with the rest of the class and say the Lord's Prayer. For most of us, it came out a bit garbled: 'Our Father which charted heaven . . .' and so on.

Most of the time, I wasn't praying, for my thoughts were elsewhere. I was simply parroting sounds.

But on some occasions I *was* praying. These were the times I thought of God, and in my own way, wanted to speak to Him. I believe those prayers, even if the words didn't always make sense, were accepted by God.

I should say, however, that our thoughts don't have to be focussed on God all the time we are praying in tongues. I often pray in tongues as I am driving a car; my concentration is on the traffic and road conditions and on handling the car, while God is in the periphery of my attention.

I often pray in tongues while listening to a sermon. I believe I may be praying for the preacher as I concentrate on what he is saying, but I have also involved God in my overall awareness of the experience.

What happens is that I yield myself to God for His Spirit to pray with my spirit, using my vocal organs (even silently, as when listening to a sermon in church) – while my mind gets on with coping with my circumstances.

Praying in the Spirit is a joint effort of both the human spirit and the Holy Spirit. If you want to be sure you are doing it – pray in tongues.


*Text references*
The list referred to in the chapter is from 1 to 23.
1. Acts 2 verse 4.
2. Acts 10 verses 44, 46.
3. Acts 19 verses 5, 6.
4. Romans 8 verses 15, 16.
5. Romans 8 verse 26.
6. Matthew 22 verses 43, 44.
7. Luke 2 verse 27.
8. Luke 4 verse 1.
9. Revelation 1 verse 10.
10. Revelation 4 verse 2.
11. Revelation 17 verse 3.
12. Revelation 21 verse 10.
13. 1 Corinthians 12 verses 7–10.
14. 1 Corinthians 12 verse 30.
15. 1 Corinthians 14 verse 5.
16. 1 Corinthians 14 verses 13–16.

17. 1 Corinthians 14 verse 19.
18. 1 Corinthians 14 verse 23.
19. 1 Corinthians 14 verses 27, 28.
20. 1 Corinthians 14 verses 32, 33.
21. 1 Corinthians 14 verse 39.
22. Ephesians 6 verses 17, 18.
23. Jude verses 19, 20.
And other texts referred to in the chapter but not included in the list:
24. Galatians 5 verses 16, 25.
25. Ephesians 1 verse 1.

# CHAPTER FOURTEEN

# Our weakness is Christ's opportunity

Since The Salvation Army dismissed us from officership, Jean and I have been under frequent Satanic attack. He has attacked us in our family life and in our thought life – in professional life and in our service for God. And I've had enough cause to feel loss of self-respect and worthlessness. Perhaps it was useful for me, anyway, because my last position as a Salvation Army officer – supervisor of SA schools in Hong Kong – could have given me false ideas of my own self-importance.

Maybe my ego had to take a bashing, but I feel Satan intended something worse – my destruction.

Even while writing this book, I've experienced Satanic attack, especially in the days leading up to publication. In fact, Satan has become almost predictable in his attacks: let something go well for me spiritually, and I know he will be after me – sometimes within hours.

Of course, good things have also happened. We've had opportunities to minister, to bless and be blessed. A wider field of service has opened up to us than we ever had before, and we've seen God working in our children and our relatives. It hasn't been hardship all the way. God has intervened, often supernaturally, and at times, it's been very easy to rejoice.

But Satan is never far away, trying to upset and spoil

things.

In all these troubles, speaking and praying in tongues has helped inspire and comfort me. When anxiety threatened, I have turned to God and found Him ever there. When depression came with its misery and the feeling of life being hopeless, it was in my relationship with Him I found solace and victory.

When we came back to Scotland from Hong Kong, we had no home nor the means of getting one, so we lived with our son, Paul, and his wife, Linda. We applied for a local authority house, and after fifteen months, because we were officially 'homeless', we reached top of the housing list.

Three bungalows were being built in a nearby village, and the housing authority said we'd get one. Because Jean had already become convinced God wanted to give us one of them, we often visited the building site to check on progress. On one occasion, she and a friend and I laid hands on a nearly-completed house and claimed it in the Name of Jesus Christ.

When they were ready for let, I called at the Housing Office. I went in with hopes high – and came out, stunned and incredulous.

It was true, we had been top of the list, but this information was mislaid between the front office and the Committee who allocated the houses. We were never considered.

Jean was shattered. It undermined her confidence in knowing God's guidance. If she had been wrong about this, could she not also be wrong about other things? Even about her relationship with God?

That was a bad time for us, but we held on, for we knew God. We had experienced Him – we had obeyed Him and seen Him do miracles. Our relationship would survive this set-back.

So we continued to trust God, and eventually His light shone through the blackness of that experience; and there came the time when we saw that good had stemmed from it.

I now see that the dark experience of life are like being manoeuvred into a corner facing inwards, so that all the perspective lines draw the eyes and the thinking towards a point. The mind is imprisoned on a treadmill of thoughts and possibilities, and for me, anxiety and depression are the outcome. But when I pray in tongues, it turns me around – out of the corner – to face Jesus.

Then the anxieties are behind me. They haven't gone away, they still exist, but they no longer block the horizon. They are scaled down to God's perspective, for beside Him, they are small indeed.

I enjoy walking in the mountains above Glen Doll, Angus-shire. High up there, all the problems of life below seem petty and unimportant. Of course, when I go back down to the lower lands, the problems still remain, but the glimpse from a higher viewpoint has helped to put them in a true perspective.

For me, praying in tongues is a glimpse of God's heights.

And I know that the Holy Spirit is praying through me, so that no matter how bad the situation or how weak I feel, when I pray in tongues, ideal prayer is being said. It may not be for me or my situation, of course, but I know that God knows best and He never makes mistakes.

Perhaps you who read this can say: 'But I never worry – I'm never anxious.'

You're fortunate then. For many of us, it takes great effort to obey the command in Philippians:

'– be careful (anxious) for nothing.'[1]

For some of us have worrying natures. Why should this be?

Various causes have been suggested, such as unhappy childhood experiences which have prepared us to expect the worst from life, or even our body chemicals being out of balance.[2] And from one or the other, or a combination of these, we develop a pessimistic way of looking at life, along with a low opinion of ourselves. Our usual perception of a situation is to see it in the worst possible light.[3]

I've found much help in a Bible promise:

' – all things work together for good to them that love God, to them who are the called according to His purpose.'[4]

When things start to go wrong, or a worrying situation develops, I remember that promise. Of course, it takes faith to rest on it, but God honours faith.

One of the difficulties of being depressed, however, is that you often don't feel worthy enough for God to promise you anything. So there may be a real blockage within yourself to prevent you laying hold of His promise. I find that problems and worries can become a smokescreen so that it takes an assertion of faith to pierce it through and see God's promise.

That's when the habit of praying in tongues is useful. Tongues has become for me a natural response to a difficult situation, and I find it breaks the cycle of depression and anxiety and helps me see God. It turns me out of the corner to face Jesus.

Then as His promise becomes real and I realise that even this situation is working out for my good so it is easy to praise and thank Him. And as I do this, depression lifts, anxiety is dispelled.

Another helpful passage from the Bible is:

*'And lest I should be exalted above measure through the abundance of the revelations, there was given to me a thorn in the flesh, the messenger of Satan to buffet me, lest I should be exalted above measure. For this thing I besought the Lord thrice, that it might depart from me. And he said unto me, My grace is sufficient for thee: for my strength is made perfect in weakness. Most gladly therefore will I rather glory in my infirmities, that the power of Christ may rest upon me. Therefore I take pleasure in infirmities, in reproaches, in necessities, in persecutions, in distresses for Christ's sake: for when I am weak, then am I strong.'*[5]

When we really possess this passage, it has a positive effect on our thinking. Instead of looking on the black side of things, instead of always being self-critical, we develop a self-respect, because we see ourselves, warts an' all, as being valuable to God. And our weakness can be a help to Jesus Christ.

Verse 9 says that Christ's 'strength is made perfect in weakness.'

In John's Gospel chapter 1 verse 3, we read that *'all things were made by Him – '* the Word of God. Jesus Christ's power was revealed in creation.

But it is in our weakness that His power is made perfect. Far from our weakness being disappointing to God, if it causes us to depend more on Him, then it glorifies Jesus.

Paul glories or boasts in his weakness, in the defects he would be happier without. And that may include defects in personality as well as physical weaknesses.

The word 'infirmity' is used for physical sickness, but it

may also be used for the infirmities of the soul, the tendencies to sin.

In writing to Rome, Paul used the word thus:

*'I speak after the manner of men because of the infirmity of your flesh –'*[6]

There it refers to our natural limitations. So the 'infirmities' in the passage from 2 Corinthians may be limitations of our bodies and our minds . . . perhaps the ones which depress you. But like Paul, you should glory in them. And why? Because Jesus Christ can display His perfect power through them.

It took power to create the universe from nothing[7] – but the universe was pliant in His hands. You have will – you can struggle and resist. You can give or withhold your love and trust, and your obedience. However, when you give Him these, when you hand the reins of your life to Him, when you relinquish your all to Him, including your weaknesses and infirmities, then His power is manifested through you in such a way that all the wonders of the universe cannot compare with it.

And when you do this, says Paul, the power of Christ rests upon you. In speaking of resting on you, he uses a word which means 'setting up a permanent dwelling place.' Christ and His power are not in transit: it's meant to be a permanent relationship.

Now do you see how you – with all your faults and weaknesses – are important to God? If you've got a low opinion of yourself – that will have to change. Remember! You are a son of God! Get your thinking in step with God's evaluation of you.

In the tenth verse, we read:

Let's take these words one at a time.

'Reproach' is both the insult, and the pain and trauma it causes you.

'Sticks and stones can break your bones, but names can never hurt you –'

Don't believe it. As one of the characters in the Charlie Brown strip-cartoon said: 'they can when they're infected'. Can you take pleasure in insults and their hurts? Paul did – so that Christ could reveal His power in him.

'Persecutions' – we find that word in the parable of the Sower, referring to the one who had no root in himself and who endured only for a while: ' *– for when tribulation or persecution ariseth because of the word, by and by he is offended.'*[8]

Persecution is when people deliberately make you suffer. It doesn't encourage self-respect to know that people dislike you that much. That can have a depressing effect on you. But when persecution comes, take pleasure in it, because in it, Christ's power is perfected.

Jesus was despised and rejected by men.[9] Have you experienced that? Or perhaps you are suffering it at this moment. Remember – the people who despise and reject you are probably in the wrong – most likely their persecution is completely unjustified.

But again – even if they're not wrong – if what they're saying about you, doing to you, is a reasonable – though un-Christian way of responding to what you've said and done – you can still get comfort from this Bible passage.

For the text doesn't say:

' – I take pleasure in persecutions I don't deserve.'

For none of us is perfect. We all make mistakes at some time; rub somebody up the wrong way just by being ourselves. We all have faults, and sometimes they get us into trouble with other people.

But we don't open ourselves up to the grace of God to get what we deserve – if we were to receive our just desserts, we would be in a sorry state. 'Grace' means 'undeserved mercy'. That's what we need, and that's what we're promised.

Paul said he took pleasure in all the persecutions which came his way, and we must do the same – regardless of whether we deserve them or not.

He also took pleasure in 'necessities'. Circumstances can cause anxiety and depression. And 'necessities' are those circumstances which are forced on us – perhaps because of our sense of responsibility or our Christian principles. Perhaps sticking to your principles gets you in bad with your employer or fellow-workers. Or by fulfilling your responsibilities, perhaps to a loved one, you have embraced a life of self-denial and suffering. These are the 'necessities' which Paul took pleasure in. For he had the God-perspective. He saw things from a loftier viewpoint.

'Distresses' is derived from 'hemmed or penned in', and not being able to extricate yourself.

Distresses crush you in, and that is when you must burst free by prayer in the Spirit and faith in God's written word. Glory in your distresses so that the power of Christ moves in you and your circumstances, and seeing it, others will praise Him.

Paul glories for Christ's sake. The Greek word 'huper' translated 'for' means 'on behalf of'. It is derived from the idea of doing something for the benefit of another.

Far from these things making you anxious or depressed, you should see them as opportunities to benefit Jesus Christ.

And what can you do about your body's chemical levels if they are the main cause of your anxiety or depression?

In 1967, I lay in bed in pain following a minor operation to remove a piece of bone from my leg for biopsy. I was sure there was nothing seriously wrong with me – just a lump below the knee. But one day, alone at home, I had a conversation with God. He started it:

'Jim, you haven't asked me to heal you.'

'Well, there isn't anything wrong with me, God.'

'Nevertheless, you should ask me to heal you.'

'All right, Lord,' I said, although I thought it unnecessary, 'All right, Lord, please heal me, in Jesus' Name.'

'Right, I will.'

About a week later, the doctor called in to see me, looking very pleased about something.

'Wonderful news,' he said. 'There's nothing wrong with your leg. It's all clear.'

Jean and I were surprised at his obvious relief.

'But of course,' I replied. 'You didn't think there was anything wrong, did you?'

And then he told us that both he and the people at the hospital had been almost certain I had cancer in the bone of my leg; all the evidence, all the symptoms, pointed to it.

I had learnt a lesson:

God heals today!

So ask God to heal you of any bio-chemical imbalance which makes you a worrier.

Earlier in this chapter I referred to a verse from Philippians.[1]

*'Be careful for nothing –'*

The word translated 'careful' means to be drawn in different directions, and is usually represented as 'anxious' or 'distracted'.

God does not want you to be anxious – or distracted – or pulled in different directions. But to be single-minded, your eyes fixed on Jesus. And when you trust that God is working in your circumstances for good, and that His strength is made perfect in your weaknesses – then you can really pray and praise Him with with thanksgiving.

Don't let Satan distract you with anxiety and depression from glorifying Jesus Christ.

When you are attacked pray in the Spirit, and think on these truths from the Bible. And change your opinion of yourself – you are a son of God – and you are valuable to Him.

*Text references*
1. Philippians 4 verse 6.
2. Leshner, A. I. (1977) 'Hormones in Emotions' in Candland D. K. et al *Emotion* Monterey: Brooks/Cole.
3. Shaw B. F. 'Cognitive Model for Depression' in Pliner et al (1979) *Perception of Emotion in Self and Others* N.Y. Plenum Press.
4. Romans 8 verse 28.
5. 2 Corinthians 12 verse 7–10.
6. Romans 6 verse 19.
7. Hebrews 11 verse 3.
8. Matthew 13 verse 21.
9. Isaiah 53 verse 3.

# CHAPTER FIFTEEN

# Love – not argument

Christians do it . . .
in the cause of Christ, they do it . . .
using the Bible, they do it . . .
to extend the Kingdom of God, they do it . . .
and yet, it's Satan's secret weapon!
What is it?
ARGUING!

Never argue. You'll meet Christians determined to prove that tongues are wrong. And naturally, you'll disagree. So you'll try to persuade them that it's they who are wrong – not the speakers in tongues.

But you can't do it. It is not possible to convince anyone against his will. He simply 'puts up the shutters'. He won't listen. While you are speaking, he'll be marshalling his own arguments – listening with 'half an ear' to you, just in case you blunder.

And you'll be listening with your half ear to him – so it cuts both ways.

I used to love arguments. I was an atheist throughout my teen years, until I was twenty-one. I loved to argue against the Christian faith – it seemed perfectly set up to be knocked down.

Even after I became a Christian, I argued. The only

difference was that I had exchanged arguing positions.

I think I began to doubt the wisdom of arguing when I was travelling in a train one day with other Salvation Army officers. It was one of those open coaches with rows of seats so it was possible for a number of people to overhear you unless you spoke quietly. Two young men, obviously keen members of the Mormons, struck up a conversation with us. They intended to convert us to their beliefs.

The question of being children of God or of the devil arose, and our beliefs were obviously at variance. And then, just after I had been holding forth about being children of wrath or disobedience until we were born again, into a moment of silence like a stone shattering the surface of a still pool, came the words of an elderly lady down the passage:

'Well, in that case I'll have no time for them in future . . .'

I do not know if she disapproved of my doctrine or of my argumentativeness, but I do know I'd lost a supporter for The Salvation Army. So I suppose it wasn't a very successful argument.

But in a way, it was – for I was learning. I was learning that arguing can turn more people off than it convinces.

When we argue, those beliefs of ours which have shaky foundations are shown to need extra propping up – or if they seem secure, then they're more solid than ever. The fact of the matter is that people won't be convinced against their will. Even if the truth is staring them in the face. Jesus referred to this stubbornness of unbelief when He said that unbelievers would not be convinced even though one rose from the dead.[1]

But for me, there is another danger in arguing. For arguing attacks my peace of mind. It has much the same effect as if I were harbouring a secret sin. Arguing leaves me feeling down. So if someone says to me:

'Speaking in tongues is wrong – it's not of God.'

I have to recognise the danger signal. Satan is waiting with his secret weapon.

So what should I do?

I will discuss.

For there is a difference between arguing and discussing.

What they have in common is that you collect your ideas and present them in as persuasive a manner as possible. But there is a difference:

In arguing, you identify yourself with your ideas. An attack on your ideas is seen as an attack on yourself. It becomes a personal thing. That is why people get worked-up in an argument.

When you discuss your beliefs in the Bible, you don't have to feel that you are under attack. It is the word of God which is being attacked. And as you don't have to defend a tiger – how much less do you have to defend the word of God.

State the truth – say what the Bible says. The Holy Spirit does the rest.

If the other person wants to argue – cool it down by asking him why he doesn't believe in tongues. And don't interrupt him. Let him give his reasons – all of them.

Then if you get the chance, put your point of view. He'll be more likely to listen if he's had his say. He'll want a rest, if nothing else. And put your point of view by asking him for his views – as for example:

'What d'you think Paul meant by saying: "So that ye come behind in no gift; waiting for the coming of our Lord Jesus Christ":'[2]

And give him all the time he wants to answer. Don't

interrupt! Remember, he could find himself arguing with God, and God convinces better than you can.

It helps to know why people argue against speaking in tongues. There may be many reasons, but there are three basic ones:

## 1. Fear

Speaking in tongues is unusual. People think it strange, even spooky. To some Christians, it looks like being possessed by strange forces and losing control of yourself.

You can't argue fear out of people. But if they see you happy and in control of yourself, despite speaking in tongues, that helps to convince them there's nothing to be frightened of. If they accept the Bible as God's word, show them the part in Acts chapter 2 where the onlookers thought speaking in tongues was strange. Yet it was of God – and still is. And if God gives this gift – then it is for our good – even if it does seem strange.

Some bystanders were probably afraid when Lazarus came out of the tomb; when fire licked up the water on Elijah's altar on Mount Carmel; on many other occasions when God's power was shown in everyday experience. But we don't reject God's power just because we don't understand it. Instead, it should make us love and respect Him more.

This fear may show itself another way: fear of doing anything which may lower the church attendance figures or reduce the membership roll. It shows itself this way:

'We don't want tongues because they are divisive. The older saints would never accept them – tongues would split the fellowship.'

'I've heard it said. More than once. By fine sincere Christians.

But can you imagine some of the leaders of the Jews saying to Jesus:

'We don't want your message because it would not be acceptable to many of the Sanhedrin and the Pharisees and Sadduccees – it would cause division. Sorry, Jesus, but unity comes first . . .'

Of course, Christians who are not in sympathy with the charismatic experience, with the benefit of hindsight disagree with those leaders of the Jews. But would they have disagreed if they had been there with them, with no hindsight, and were concerned mainly with maintaining peace and unity at any price?

As a leader of a Christian group said to me recently in defence of their anti-tongues stance in order to maintain unity:

'We don't look to the Scriptures for support of our view, but rather to the needs of the situation . . .'

That's what fear does . . .


## 2. Jealousy

Sometimes, Christians are jealous of others speaking in tongues. Does that sound reasonable? Well, see it this way. These Christians may have served God faithfully for years, often without a great deal of enjoyment, perhaps with little to show for all their sacrifice. Then along comes a new Christian – someone who doesn't know the Bible very well, isn't strict with himself about what he does on Sundays or about the length of his hair, or always laughing and joking, isn't particular about some of the company he keeps – and he starts off speaking in tongues and witnessing and praising the Lord and leading souls to the Lord. And it just doesn't seem fair. If anyone is going to be filled with the Spirit and have His gifts, it should be the Christians who

132

are sober and respectable and have adorned the Gospel over the years, not these puffed-up, fly-by-night new converts.

That makes sense, doesn't it? It would have to the Pharisees and doctors of the law when they saw a man from despised Galilee being hailed as the Messiah.[3]

But God does not work by our standards. He chooses the humble and simple and weak things of the world.[4] And perhaps, if we know we are humble and simple and weak, and our virtues and strong points are nothings alongside Him, then we are in the right condition to be blessed and used. Who knows, that may be why God sometimes chooses new Christians and fills them with His Spirit . . .

So fear and jealousy can create hostility to speaking in tongues. There is the third basic cause of the anti-charismatic attitude to consider:

### 3. Misunderstanding the Bible

It is true that 1 Corinthians 13 verse 8 says – 'tongues shall cease'. And the list of gifts in 1 Corinthians 12 has tongues, but the later list in Ephesians chapter 3 hasn't. And tongues is second last in the Corinthian list, and Paul says he would rather have us prophesy than speak in tongues.

*But they don't add up to: 'Tongues is wrong!'*

We have already looked at the first two of these passages. Regarding the other two:

We must remember that no gift from God is unimportant, even if it does come second last in a list. 'Meekness' and 'temperance' are the last two items in the list of the fruit of the Spirit – but who says they are unimportant?[5]

And when tongues are interpreted, they, like prophecy, edify the church.[6]

133

When someone says tongues is wrong, listen to his reasons. Satan doesn't want that Christian to be blessed with this gift, or through its use, to bless others. Satan is the enemy. Not the Christian who disagrees with you.

Lovingly share with him your experience and the Biblical evidence for it. But don't argue!

Once he sees that speaking in tongues benefits you, he will be interested. Most Christians want the power of God in their lives; they want to be more Christlike. If they see that being filled with the Spirit of God and having the gifts of the Spirit, including tongues, does that for you, they'll want the experience too.

I read somewhere recently that many charismatic Christians are better at explaining about the gifts of the Spirit than showing them. What the church needs today is not so much explanation, but more demonstration. Prejudice against the charismatic position, will not be argued away, but when people see the gifts in action, they'll be convinced they are of God.

*'Truly the signs of an apostle were wrought among you in all patience, in signs and wonders, and mighty deeds.'*[7]

(And in case you think: 'But "apostle" refers only to a chosen few who witnessed the resurrection of Christ, and so on,' just note that Paul used the word "apostle" referring not only to himself, but also to Silvanus and Timothy.[8])

We charismatic Christians must beware in case we make tongues an end in itself – or even make being filled with the Holy Spirit an end in itself. It is not the end! It is not our goal!

But it is the equipping with the Holy Spirit and His power to help us move towards that end, towards that goal – to doing God's will in His way to His glory.

An argument does not reflect the love of God. Or the power of the Holy Spirit. It is as if we were trying to force something which can only be done by God. Let the Holy Spirit do the persuading.

Often when I find myself in a discussion with someone who is opposed to the use of the gifts of the Spirit today, I find myself praying in tongues quietly within myself, even as I listen. And praying in English, too. It's an effective exercise, for apart from its effect on the other, it keeps me sweet . . .

It is dangerously easy to forget that the Christian who is against tongues is a brother in Christ – not a bother in Christ. He is a fellow-member of the Body of Christ. And we are bound together in a spiritual unity.

Some years ago, a ministers' fraternal I was a member of, planned a joint service for church unity, and I was invited to preach. I thought about it and prayed, and there came to me fresh insight I hadn't considered before: it was that we Christians don't have to strive for unity – God's Spirit has already baptised us all into the Body of Christ,[9] we are already united.

What we have to do is to recognise and acknowledge that unity. We are one in Christ. Let us live it out. And where some speak in tongues, and others don't – that need not cause separation – disunity – the break-up of Christ's Body on earth.

All Christians – charismatic and anti-charismatic (and non-charismatic) have a heavy responsibility – for if there is a splintering of the Body of Christ, we are all to blame. And the Body does splinter – if we don't care sufficiently.

But if we are prepared to discuss our differences, to pray

together – to *'speak the truth in love'*[10] – not in order to score points but in order to help each other grow in Christ – then we all *'may grow up into him in all things, which is the head, even Christ.'*[10]

*Text references*
1. Luke 16 verse 31.
2. 1 Corinthians 1 verse 7.
3. John 7 verse 52.
4. 1 Corinthians 1 verse 27.
5. Galatians 5 verses 22, 23.
6. 1 Corinthians 14 verse 5.
7. 2 Corinthians 12 verse 12.
8. 1 Thessalonians 2 verse 6, and 1 verse 1.
9. 1 Corinthians 12 verse 13.
10. Ephesians 4 verse 15.

# CHAPTER SIXTEEN

# ' – be filled with the Spirit'

Now we are at the last chapter, let me ask the question:

'Have you been filled with the Holy Spirit and spoken in tongues?'

If you have, then this chapter isn't really for you, although you may find it useful for helping others.

But to other readers who have never been filled with the Spirit and spoken in tongues, then allow me to explain how you can have this experience.

First, make sure you are a Christian. Do you know you need to be saved from sin?

Sin is not merely the big wrong-doings – like murder and theft and adultery – or even the smaller wrongs, like telling 'white lies' or 'borrowing' things from your work-place, or cheating the taxman – but sin is not doing God's will for your life.

*'All have sinned and come short of the glory of God –'*[1] And 'all' means everyone.

*'He has made him (Jesus), who knew no sin, to be sin for us, that we might be made the righteousness of God in him.'*[2]

And if we confess our sins, and trust in His sacrifice to save us – we will be forgiven.[3]

Get your sins dealt with, then invite Jesus into your life as your Lord and Saviour.[4]

Pray to God – something along these lines – but make sure the words are real for yourself:

'Heavenly Father, please forgive my sins – for now I trust in Jesus Christ and His sacrifice to save me from my sin. And Jesus, I now ask you to come into my life to be my Lord and Saviour. I will trust and depend entirely and only on you, Jesus, to make and keep me right with God.'

Asking forgiveness for sins, then inviting Christ into your life is like having the house cleaned for an important guest, except you ask the guest to clean it for you because you can't do it yourself.

Once you do this, you may be filled with the Holy Spirit. And it can happen at once. You don't have to wait for a period of instruction or approval by the Church.

In Caesarea on the Mediterranean coast of Palestine lived the Centurion, Cornelius with his friends. They were keen adherents of the Jewish faith, but they wanted to find out about Jesus, so they sent to Joppa for Simon Peter to come and instruct them.

Peter went to them and told them of Jesus' death and resurrection, and at the point where he said of Jesus that:

' – *through His name whosoever believeth in Him shall receive remission of sins –* '[5]

the Holy Sprit fell on them and they all spoke in tongues. They became Christians and were filled with the Holy Spirit at the same time. And that is how it can be for you.

On the other hand, if you are already a Christian, then the promise of the Spirit is for you now, because God has no favourites.

*'If ye then, being evil, know how to give good gifts unto your children: how much more shall your heavenly Father give the Holy Spirit to them that ask Him?'*[6]

God wants you to be filled with the Holy Spirit more than you want it. But a warning!

Most people have dabbled in the spirit world at some time, and not with God's Spirit either. They've done it through superstitious practices, or relying on good luck charms or horoscopes or tea-leaves readings or such-like, or even through tarot cards, ouija boards, seances and spiritualist meetings. But however it was done, you've been opened to other-spirit influences, and before you invite the Holy Spirit to fill you, you must renounce these other things. Say something like this:

'I renounce you – (and here name whatever you've been involved in) – I will have no more to do with you. I give you up – I have done with you completely – in the Name of Jesus Christ.'

Done that? Now receive the Holy Spirit.

And as you receive Him, so be open to His taking over your tongue. Perhaps you are apprehensive, but don't be, for God loves you.

You may be thinking: 'Shall I pray? Should I praise and thank God? But then I'd be speaking in English.'

Don't be concerned. You praise and thank Him if you feel you have to.

But don't let your English speech deafen your inner ear so that you don't hear, or are not sensitive to, the Spirit's prompting.

An almost inarticulate sound forms in your mind. Nonsense sound? Say it out loud. By faith, say it.

Remember, not by your understanding but by your spirit – you pray in tongues. He gives the utterance – you speak it out.[7]

So say that nonsense syllable. Be a fool for Christ. Say it out – don't whisper it. Nowhere in the Bible do we read they whispered in tongues. They may have done so – but all we read about are those who spoke it out loud. Paul told the Corinthians to be prepared to speak in tongues within themselves – and so should you, when the occasion demands it – but now is not such an occasion. Now is the time to speak aloud.[8]

Keep on doing it, even if it is only one sound. Even if it sounds ridiculous. In faith – believe it is from God. Obey His prompting. And do it to please God.

I used to pray in tongues looking at myself in the bathroom mirror, because it helped me come to terms with my self-consciousness. It sounded so foolish. But I did it for God, and He blessed me.

Some Christian may say:

'I've tried and tried in the past – and it's never worked for me. God doesn't want me to have tongues – to be filled with His Spirit.'

If you know you haven't been filled with the Spirit and haven't prayed in tongues, no one can dispute your experience.

But the conclusion you draw from it contradicts God's word.

He does want you to be filled with His Spirit.

Ephesians 5 verse 18 commands you to:

' – *be not drunk with wine, wherein is excess; but be filled with the Spirit.*'

That is a command. And what is more, it really means:

'– go on continually being filled with the Spirit.'

And again in Ephesians, we read that we all should put on the whole armour of God and should be:

'– praying always with all prayer and supplication in the Spirit –'⁹

Whatever else that may mean, it certainly means praying in tongues.

So don't say that you're excluded from these commands or instructions.

If God wants you to be filled with the Spirit and to pray in tongues – and you've tried to obey Him – and it hasn't happened for you – what then?

There are two possible explanations:

Either you have been filled with the Holy Spirit, but something is blocking your tongues –

or

Something is blocking your being filled with the Spirit. There is a blockage somewhere. So let's find it and deal with it by God's help.

I was ministering one Sunday in a church, when a young woman, a scientist, came forward for prayer to be filled with the Holy Spirit. Apparently she had often done this in the past but it never seemed to work for her. So I laid hands on her and prayed. Nothing happened. I prayed again then left her while I ministered to another. When I returned, she shook her head: 'Nothing! It doesn't work.'

I prayed inside myself, asking God for guidance, and into my thoughts came: 'Her scientific training and outlook is blocking it.'

So I asked her if this was so and she thought for a few

moments, then smiled. 'That's it,' she agreed. 'I just can't accept that speaking in tongues is scientific.'

'Are you prepared to put aside scientific attitudes and values when we're on the things of the Spirit? After all, science is not equipped for dealing with God.'

She didn't hesitate. 'I'll do it,' she agreed.

She bowed her head and prayed, and within seconds, she was praying quietly in tongues and gradually getting louder. I heard recently she has started a Charismatic prayer meeting for her Christian colleagues.

There is something we ought to be sure about here before we go any further: When it comes to God's grace – He takes the initiative!

Our part is to respond to Him.

'– while we were yet sinners, Christ died for us.'[10]

God leads – we follow.

If you want to be filled with the Holy Spirit, that's because God has created that need within you. Jesus said that the Holy Spirit would guide us into all truth.[11] It is He Who reveals spiritual things to us,[12] so that our desire to be filled with the Spirit and have His gifts, including tongues, comes from God. As long as you don't want it for your own selfish ends.[13]

If you have doubts about your motives, tell God about it. He already knows of course, but He wants us to speak to Him about everything. So tell Him. And ask Him to help you have the right motives. Then leave that problem with Him. Your submission and faith gives God the opportunity to work in you.

Things from our past can block the blessing.

Jean, our daughter Ruth, and I, were praying with one of our sons, Mark, who had been into drugs before he

142

became a Christian. He wanted to be filled with the Holy Spirit, but nothing happened when we prayed and laid hands on him. It was suggested that evil spirits which had access into him in his drug-taking days were still there.

But I couldn't agree that evil spirits had any part in a Christian, though Jean and Ruth and Mark did. We continued in prayer, but there was no breakthrough. Then Mark said that while we prayed, a voice within him was saying:

'Ha, ha – I've nothing to fear here. He doesn't believe.'

And the 'he' referred to me. I felt resentful, so I quickly brought it to God and claimed the protection of the blood of Jesus Christ.

Jean left the room for a few minutes, and when she returned, she said: 'You're not fully persuaded about this, Jim, so I will accept your ruling.'

But God had already spoken to me. 'No, Jean, I accept that evil spirits may still oppress Christians in areas of their lives not surrendered to God.'

So we agreed and took authority against the evil spirits. We commanded them to go, and Mark felt immediate release and freedom. Later that evening, he prayed in tongues, and his prayer language became a channel of God's blessing into his own life, and through him, to others.

It is important to remember that our actions in the past may have allowed evil spirits to oppress us, and they can thereafter block God's blessing unless they're dealt with. And sometimes the actions of loved ones can also create a blockage in us.

The other day I heard of a baby who was 'christened' in a spiritualist church meeting, and a spirit named 'Arnold' was invited to look after the child from then on. That kind of blockage could deprive that child of God's blessing in later years.

But remember, Jesus is greater than Satan and all his spirits.

*'Greater is He that is in you, than he that is in the world.'*

*'Submit yourselves therefore to God. Resist the devil, and he will flee from you.'*[14]

If you command evil spirits to go, and you use the Name of Jesus Christ and the protection of His Blood they must go.

'Lord, I claim the protection of the blood of Jesus Christ, and I command you evil spirit, in the Name and authority of Jesus Christ, to get out now and go to your own place. Now, go!'

It is best, however, to get Spirit-filled Christians to join with you in this, if you can. But if you can't, then do it by yourself.

What other blockages are there to being filled with the Holy Spirit?

I believe that membership of a society which involves vows of secrecy can be a blockage. Why? Because your vow becomes a binding fetter on your life, even stronger than your loyalty to God. It makes an area of your life where God is not supreme – where He does not have the deciding word. Have done with it – assert Christ's lordship over all your life. That doesn't mean you go round telling everything you know about that society. However, if it is true, as has been claimed,[15,16] that Freemasonry acknowledges Lucifer as god, the Christian must recognize that he owes Lucifer/Satan nothing – not even silence.

Ask the Holy Spirit to show you anything in your

thoughts which may be a barrier. It could be a scientific-rational attitude: or a bias against tongues, inherited from parents or church; or the fear of looking ridiculous, even to yourself; or an inferiority complex which makes you think you're not good enough for the Holy Spirit to work through you; or a very critical attitude, always looking for faults, even with God.

Whatever God reveals to you, turn over to Him. Ask forgiveness and healing in the name of Jesus Christ. Then abandon yourself to God and let Him work in you.

Perhaps God has reminded you of a resentment from years ago, or from more recently. Turn it over to God. Forgive whoever hurt you. Don't nurse a grievance or it will make you spiritually sick.

If you've wronged someone, do whatever the Holy Spirit tells you. Put it right with them – or leave it with God. Perhaps it must be dealt with later. Or it may be even now too late – the wronged one may have died. If that is so, then leave the wrong you have done under the blood of Jesus.

Having dealt with the blockages, ask God to fill you with His Spirit and expect Him to do so.

Often when I bring a message in tongues or in English from God, I get only one word or sound, but as I launch out believing God's Spirit is doing it, He provides the sounds and words. The order in which it happens is this:

First, I have the conviction God wants to speak through me. A voice in my thoughts tells me to speak: it may be likened to a radio operator being told to get ready to transmit a message.

Within myself, I ask this voice to confess that Jesus Christ is come in the flesh.[17] But the longer I walk with God and the more I obey Him, the more easily I recognise His voice.

After I'm sure it is from God, I yield my vocal organs to

145

make the sound or word or whatever was forming in my mind. It has to be an act of my will, for I'm in control of my vocal organs all the time, as the Bible says:

'– the spirits of the prophets are subject to the prophets.'[18]

So there it is. I have no more to say. Will you now receive the Holy Spirit and speak in tongues? You can – do it now.

May the Lord bless you richly, and in using you, make you a channel of blessing to others.

*Text references*
  1. Romans 3 verse 23.
  2. 2 Corinthians 5 verse 21.
  3. 1 John 1 verse 9.
  4. John 1 verse 12; Revelation 3 verse 20.
  5. Acts 10 verse 43.
  6. Luke 11 verse 13.
  7. Acts 2 verse 4.
  8. 1 Corinthians 14 verse 28.
  9. Ephesians 6 verse 18.
 10. Romans 5 verse 8.
 11. John 16 verse 13.
 12. 1 Corinthians 2 verses 11, 12, 14.
 13. Acts 8 verses 18 to 24.
 14. 1 John 4 verse 4; James 4 verse 7.
 15. S. Knight (1985) *The Brotherhood*. London: Granada Publishing. Chapter 25.
 16. W. J. McK. McCormick (1984) *Christ, the Christian and Freemasonry*. Belfast: Great Joy Publications. Page 94.
 17. 1 John 4 verse 2.
 18. 1 Corinthians 14 verse 32.

# Appendix

# Appendix

Tables extracted from unpublished Honours Thesis, University of Hong Kong, January, 1972.

*Phonemic Analysis of Glossolalia*
by Jim Davidson (1972)

<table>
<tr><td colspan="2" align="center">Table 1<br>Judges' nationalities and languages of fluency<br>in preliminary study</td></tr>
<tr><td>Nationality</td><td>Language fluent in</td></tr>
<tr><td>(1) USA</td><td>American, English</td></tr>
<tr><td>(2) Panama</td><td>Spanish, English, Mandarin</td></tr>
<tr><td>(3) Dominican Rep.</td><td>Spanish</td></tr>
<tr><td>(4) Switzerland</td><td>German, French, Italian, English</td></tr>
<tr><td>(5) Philippines</td><td>English, French, Spanish</td></tr>
<tr><td>(6) Philippines</td><td>Spanish, Portuguese, Latin, English, French</td></tr>
<tr><td>(7) Venezuela</td><td>Spanish, French, English, Italian</td></tr>
<tr><td>(8) Austria</td><td>German, English</td></tr>
<tr><td>(9) France</td><td>French</td></tr>
<tr><td>(10) Germany</td><td>German, Spanish, French, Russian, English, Malay</td></tr>
<tr><td>(11) Morocco</td><td>Spanish, English, French, Arabic, Hebrew, Russian</td></tr>
<tr><td>(12) South Africa</td><td>Afrikaans, English</td></tr>
<tr><td>(13) Australia</td><td>English, German, Cantonese</td></tr>
<tr><td colspan="2">Note: The first language listed is the Judge's native language</td></tr>
</table>

### Table 2

General comments and Judges who made them
– in preliminary study

| Comments | Judges |
|---|---|
| Some utterances reminded Judges of particular languages | 1:5:6:7:8:9:10:11 |
| Glossolalia sounds like poetry | 5:7:11:12 |
| S.2 – 'shura' – American origin (S.2 was Cantonese female) | 1 |
| S.1 – 'caramanta' – Spanish or Italian (S.1 was English female) | 10 |
| 'Mantiia' appearing in different utterances | 10 |
| Utterances may not be languages | 7 |
| Utterances – not languages – composition of vowel-consonants | 10 |
| Some speakers very emotional | 12 |
| Utterances may be praying | 7 |
| Utterances have musical rhythm | 11 |

### Table 3
#### Frequency of various findings in '2–0–1' study

| Sequence | Cantonese Judges = 72 | English Judges = 29 | USA Judges = 55 |
|---|---|---|---|
| 2–0–1 | 1 | 2 | 45 |
| 2–0–0 | 2 | 7 | 7 |
| 2–1–0 | 3 | 1 | 0 |
| 1–0–1 | 9 | 3 | 1 |
| 1–1–1 | 10 | 0 | 0 |
| 1–1–0 | 3 | 5 | 0 |
| 1–0–0 | 16 | 7 | 0 |
| 0–0–1 | 6 | 0 | 0 |
| 0–1–0 | 4 | 1 | 0 |
| 0–1–1 | 2 | 1 | 0 |
| 0–0–0 | 16 | 0 | 0 |
| 2–1–1 | 0 | 2 | 2 |
| Totals | 72 | 29 | 55 |

*Notes on Table 3*

The '2–0–1' Table (Table 3) refers as follows:

'2' = nationalities of two non-speakers identified when speaking reassembled tongues

'0' = nationality of subject when praying in tongues not identified

'1' = but her nationality identified when she spoke her reassembled tongues

The significant finding for this study is the '2–0–1' result.

| Table 4 | |
|---|---|
| Diphthongs occurring in French priests' tongues | |
| Diphthong | Frequency |
| a i | 3 |
| ii e | 4 |
| ii a | 4 |
| ii o | 3 |
| ii ou | 5 |
| ii aa | 1 |
| o u | 38 |

Note: Four of the diphthongs of this Glossolalia, totalling 13 usages, are not found in French. Each has a glide from the high front vowel (ii). The fifth diphthong with a glide from (ii) is found in the French: 'il y a'.

| Total stressed syllables | Table 5 | Prepausal stressed syllables |
|---|---|---|
| 36 | – Glossolalia – | 0 |
| 39 | – French prayer – | 9 |

# Index

# INDEX

157